"Tonya's life really is a *Chicken Soup for the Soul®* story. It is inspirational, and it proves what I know to be true—that no matter where you start, you can create a life of both success and significance. I love this book, and I promise you will too!"

—JACK CANFIELD
  Co-creator of the *Chicken Soup for the Soul®* series
  and author of *The Success Principles™*

IN HIGH
HEELS
ON A
LADDER

IN HIGH HEELS ON A LADDER

THE 7 POWER TOOLS FOR DESIGNING YOUR OWN LIFE

TONYA COMER

Allentown, PA

Published by Moe Sass Publishing, Allentown, Pennsylvania

ISBN (paperback): 979-8-9861200-2-7
ISBN (hardcover): 979-8-9861200-0-3
ISBN (ebook): 979-8-9861200-1-0

Library of Congress Cataloging-in-Publication Data had
been filed for and in progress at time of printing.

Printed in the United States of America

DEDICATION PAGE

To my Mama.

I honor you for the unquestionably resourceful, relentlessly dedicated, passionately curious, fiercely unstoppable, and courageously powerful woman you are; and for the bold stand you have been for my success. I am who I am because you first stood for me. I love you. This book is for you.

To my beloved sister.

It's because of our tender moments shared together, your laughter, your wit, your fierceness, your generosity, your open-mindedness, and your light that I must continue. It is in your honor that I answer the call on my life, and I say "Yes" to service. On my darkest days and weaker moments, I will remember this promise to you. I will shake it off and get back to work because you are worth it. May you rest in peace, my dear sister. I got it from here. I hold you in my heart where there is so much room to love you. This book is for you, Boo.

Contents

Welcome to the Journey . . .

HELLO GORGEOUS!

I want to take you on a journey with me, an amazing journey to experience something you probably never imagined possible. On this journey, you will learn what it means to stand in your wholeness, live your truth, and be all that you were born to be. Before we go there, let me share a little background and what you can expect along this journey.

To function best in my professional career as an interior designer, I had to learn to survive the sexism, ageism, and stereotype of designers commonly held by the construction trades. So, fitting in while standing out was a necessary means to an end.

Here's a typical scenario. During a meeting with a new group of contractors on a job site, I'd eventually find myself performing some magic tricks with a tape measure, relying on the extra height I would gain from my high heels. And, as if there was a cue card to direct my comedic timing, I interjected a tongue-in-cheek comment, "I can do anything you can do while holding a power tool, wearing high heels, and standing on a ladder."

This usually brought laughter and some side chatter—lightening the mood and winning me favor with the guys.

See, it is true that I can handle most power tools. I am also privy to the sacred language of the trades, and I can negotiate a ladder in high heels. I am after all a tomboy at heart and my mother's child—that woman could get most household chores done with a wrench and brute force. But that show I did . . . the tape measure, the high heels, the power tool, the ladder . . . was part of my schtick, a charade. It was a preemptive maneuver, a way to be perceived as creditable by men who may have otherwise dismissed me as "just another interior designer." At least that's what I told myself.

What's truer is that underneath that façade, I felt like a fraud—an impostor. And I contrived that situation not to survive in a man's world, but rather to survive in mine. In my world, I was deeply afraid to be "found out." I held tight my secret that I felt insignificant and insecure. This was so until the day came when I hit rock bottom.

To rebuild my life after that brutal fall, I turned my life upside down, inside out, and all around. What I found was a healing path that transformed my life and revealed my truth. I tell it all in this book, *In High Heels on a Ladder: The 7 Power Tools for Designing Your Life.*

The high heels, the ladder, the power tools have a whole new meaning in this work. I hope to inspire you to look behind your own façade and do your inner work to heal and transform your life. I call this the "journey to wholeness." The journey is preemptive in that the work prepares you for living a life defined by your truth. But unlike my little charade, there is nothing fabricated about it . . . it is not some power trip or intended to elude something. On this journey, the high heels represent strength, the ladder represents the upward movement toward truth, and the 7 Power Tools are tools of transformation that help navigate the path.

I developed the 7 Power Tools by trial and error after assessing the effectiveness of my first-hand experiences with traditional therapy, emotional intelligence training, and the various methods and practices introduced to me by life coaches and spiritual teachers. Since 2009, I have been on a personal growth path, committed to making the breakthroughs in healing and awareness required for my life. When I learned how to use the 7 Power Tools in my own transformational toolkit, I began to live my best life. And this stuff is just too good to keep to myself. So, Gorgeous, I have to share it with you.

I am not a clinical therapist or an expert in psychology. I am a LIFEdesign coach, and I have helped others who found themselves stuck in life by guiding them through the healing practices that I share with you in this book. Think of me as your "spiritual sister," someone who cares enough to show you the way down and the way through on the wholeness journey. And know that I am with you.

Please, I ask that you not just read this book. Participate fully in your transformation by studying the guidance and completing the practical exercises I offer you at the end of each chapter. The 7 Power Tools are organized to build your understanding and awareness as you move through your journey. Each chapter features:

- An introductory frame to explain the Power Tool referenced in the chapter,

- My narrative, which grounds my relationship to and learning regarding the Power Tool,

- A guidance section about the Power Tool, and

- A discovery and practice session referred to as the "Journey to Wholeness Design Space." This space is sacred, designed especially for you. Here, you will use the tools as a guide to doing YOUR inner work on your journey to wholeness.

This book is a call to action—to go inward to heal your delicate inner parts which need some tender loving care. And ultimately, I hope you are inspired to take that same love out into the world to satisfy whatever is the calling for your life.

And this is my favorite part: when you are your absolute best, I get to be my absolute best. When you succeed, I succeed. When you heal, I heal. The same is true in reverse. When I am my absolute best, you get to be your absolute best. When I succeed, you succeed. When I heal, you heal. Our stories may be different, but we are united. You will come to see this when you intimately connect with this book.

So, Gorgeous, when we—you and I—stop playing small and unite in our wholeness, the strength of our feminine energy, and the power of our love, we can do great things . . . maybe even cause a Global Love Revolution which can lead to the proverbial "world peace."

So, let's get started on the journey together!

With all my love,

Tonya "Toni" Comer

Your Spiritual Sister on your Journey to Wholeness

P.S. The message in this book is intended to empower the rise of feminine energy and leadership by inspiring a movement of love. In this spirit, I use pronouns historically associated with women. This is not intended to diminish or overlook any and all readers who may find value in completing the wholeness journey and joining the Global Love Revolution. The steps in this journey to wholeness apply to all and benefit all. Come. Join. Experience. Grow. This is a movement of love; all are welcome to be a part of it, no matter how you may define, realize, or identify your gender and sexual orientation.

The
Path to
Wholeness

There are times when you may feel like an actor in a costume trying to keep your mask in place while delivering a star performance. You do all the right things—dress the part, play the role. But behind the mask, you may feel like a mismatch to the confident superstar on stage, like a fraud, questioning if you are good enough or worthy. You are deeply afraid to slip out of character, fearing that people will discover who you really are and see your insecurity, self-doubt, and shame. Even though you have arrived at a level of status and esteem in your roles in life, you feel dissatisfied, as if something is missing. Could it be that the missing thing is right there, hiding in plain sight?

Once upon a time on my world's stage, the script of my life played out quite like that. For all appearances, I was living the dream. Yet, I felt dissatisfied and out of touch with my success . . . even ashamed of my accomplishments. Life started to feel brutal, wearing down my spirit. I did everything I could to hold it all together, but it seemed the universe was indifferent to my struggle.

Being named one of the Top 20 African American Interior Designers in America was part and parcel of the gift-wrapped package I presented to the world. I did my utmost to survive in that environment and fit in seamlessly wherever I went. My life was a whirlwind of achievements, awards, and meetings with A-listers and power players. As a girl who had grown up in a government housing project and climbed the success ladder to be a top interior designer, I was now sitting at the table with the big-leaguers. And I had earned my place. I had leveraged my God-given gifts to propel my successful career climb. I carried myself with confidence and could shift the energy in a room simply by walking in with a smile—or so they told me. Still, this outer salve was no salvation for the pain and desperation I felt. I was race-walking in high heels, trying to stay one step ahead of the moment when I'd feel like a loser and a fraud once again . . . until the day when I had to confront my shame and self-doubt full on.

THE EGG ON MY FACE

It was 10:58 p.m. on the Eve of Halloween after a perfect night out. Dressed in a fitted floor-length black ball gown and five-inch black high-heeled sandals, I had just played my part in supporting one of Philadelphia's nonprofit organizations. This grand event, their annual black-tie gala and fundraiser, was not to be missed. Side by side with the city's social and political elite, we danced to one of Philly's finest bands, dined on the best cuisine, and raised money for programs designed to empower people in underserved communities. On my ten-minute drive home, my sweet tooth was clamoring for attention. Not wanting to disappoint it, I decided to stop at the neighborhood convenience store.

Surprisingly, the store was popular that night. Ribbons of red taillights illuminated the darkness as cars lined up at the gas pumps. The drivers negotiating for spots in the congested parking lot reminded me of the frog characters in the iconic 1980s arcade game Frogger.

Halloween revelers milled about in gruesome masks and painted faces. Some filled their tanks and others poured into the convenience store as if they were about to be handed free passes to Disney World.

After circling the building, I spotted an open parking space next to a six-inch-high curbed bed of grass dividing the parking lot from the drive to the back of the building. It was a comfortable temperature, somewhere in the low sixties, so I didn't mind the walk to the front door. Grabbing my tiny clutch purse from the front passenger seat, I stepped out of the car, careful not to let my heels dig into the grass. Adjusting my ball gown, I locked the car and gracefully strolled into the store as if I were walking the red carpet.

The aroma of fresh pastry filled the air. And, as luck would have it, a staff person was putting trays of warm donuts in the clear plastic self-serve case. I waited patiently as he neatly arranged each row.

While waiting, I couldn't help being amused by the wide variety of entertaining costumed 'characters' in the store that night. In walked a Johnny Depp/Edward Scissorhands look alike, except for the different wacky hairstyle. His jet-black hair with blond roots was styled in a spiky three-inch mohawk. Thick black eyeshadow decorated his eyelids. Dressed in all black, his knee-length black trench coat hung open to reveal a black T-shirt fitted to his slender body. Silver buckles ran down the lower leg of his black pants. His ankle-high, silver-toed black boots, worn loosely, flapped around his legs as he moved. I was impressed by how put together he looked in his costume. But, for all I knew, this could have been his everyday Goth garb—better yet, his everyday mask.

He hustled through the store to find his buddy, standing out of my view at the soda fridge. I could hear him grumbling loudly, "Dude, what the f&%k? Do you want Coke or Sprite? Sheesh. Make a damn decision!"

I chuckled. It was a relatable experience, having had my fair share of indecisive moments when rushed by my friends. And times when I was the one doing the rushing.

I was curious about all this activity. *Who are these people? Where are they going? How did they all decide to stop at this convenience store before going to wherever they were headed next?*

Finally, the case was stocked. I exchanged pleasantries with the staff person and thanked him for providing my evening sugar rush. With a slight grin, he replied, "No problem. Enjoy the donuts."

Grabbing waxed tissue and a pastry bag, I mulled over which donuts had the most consistent shape and the perfect amount of glaze, and chose one. On impulse, I reached for another tissue, grabbed a second donut, and placed it in the bag, too.

At one of the two cash registers, a vampire, a clown, a witch, and some sort of superhero were standing single file like elementary school kids in the lunch line. I got in place behind them. This would have to be the only night of the year where a woman wearing a ball gown, buying ninety-nine cent donuts, could stand nonchalantly in line with a motley crew of partiers.

When I reached the cashier, we exchanged pleasantries; and then she pointed to the costumed people outside the window and said, "By any chance, are you going to the same place they're going?"

I belted out a laugh. "Maybe I should," I said, and gave her a big smile.

Donuts in hand, I slid my change into my oh-so-tiny purse and strolled out of the store. Loud peals of laughter echoed through the chamber created by the adjacent brick buildings. As I turned the corner, a pickup truck full of boisterous young people sped past me, and soon I understood: my SUV was coated with at least a dozen raw eggs. "F*%k You, Bitch!" was the last thing I remember.

This "Mischief Night" prank was fun for the neighborhood rascals; but to me, it was far from funny. I was humiliated and degraded . . . *Why my car? Why meeeee?!*

As I watched the exploded eggs slide down the vertical surfaces of my car, tears streamed down my cheeks and I felt myself sinking into an abyss of darkness—the kind of place where only vampires, ghosts, goblins, and witches belonged.

This was the moment when my own mask fell off and my insecurity, shame, and self-doubt came spilling out of the seams of my costume. How ironic that my mask would fall off on a day when it is most accepted to wear a mask. All the efforts I'd made just to hold it together had been undone in minutes by a few young pranksters and a dozen raw eggs.

It felt like egg on my face. It felt personal. And I was in no shape emotionally to deal with one more personal attack.

THE ROCK BOTTOM

You see, on the outside I looked well put together—all decked out in my black label gown, shiny designer shoes, and showy handbag. On the inside, though, I was drowning in pain and fear from the recent separation from my husband. I was also on the brink of financial ruin and having a serious stare-down with a demon called Bankruptcy. One more flawed financial move and the demon would have won. On top of that, I was dealing with a mysterious medical condition exacerbated by the emotional pain, loneliness, and sense of loss I was feeling. I longed for something to relieve the pain, but my best efforts to break free from my emotional cage of self-pity hadn't helped. My self-limiting beliefs were the padlock, and my mindset of hopelessness and helplessness became my unbearable cellmates.

I was embarrassed that I had not succeeded in living up to my own expectations, and I was terrified that the future was not going to be any brighter. I didn't have the emotional capacity for one more thing to go wrong. So, I stood there in the parking lot clutching a bag of donuts while wearing a ball gown as mascara-filled tears blackened the already dark shadows under my eyes. I watched helplessly as eggs made abstract art out of my car.

Right there, in the convenience store parking lot, I hit rock bottom.

THE LIFELINE

I was exhausted, feeling utterly defeated, lifeless. Desperate for help, I laid in bed that night wondering what and who could be my lifeline. In my most vulnerable of moments, I was still trying to protect my carefully crafted persona. *Who could I expose my tender underbelly to when I'd portrayed myself as a superwoman? Who could I trust to accept me as I am, not who I have presented myself to be all these years?* To do so would be to admit I'd been wearing a mask all along, confirming that my life had been one long masquerade party. In this darkest of dark night moments, this underlying belief rose its ugly head: *Maybe I just don't matter.*

Speaking my "truth" to a total stranger on a street corner held more appeal than the idea of picking up the phone to confess to a friend. It felt safer. While I didn't completely hide my vulnerabilities from my closest friends, I was afraid of having a full-on, in-your-face confrontation with even my besties. I was sure that the mask I wore made me opaque to my friends . . . hard to see through and hard to read. Who was I fooling? They knew better. It was me who couldn't see myself and my life for what it really was. I was ashamed to realize that even my besties could probably see through me to those tender parts that I wanted to hide. But I couldn't let them know that I felt like a colossal failure. *Who could possibly love me through these times, and still like me if the storms ever passed?*

For some inexplicable reason, I thought of Katie.

I had met Katie in August—months before Halloween Eve—at a networking event. She later invited me to a presentation that her firm was giving to introduce a premium coaching program designed for business owners and senior leadership in corporate careers. Something about Katie drew me to her. So, I said "yes" to the invitation.

At our first meeting, I felt a certain kinship with Katie that I couldn't explain. Her salt and pepper hair was styled in a pixie cut that suited her well-proportioned face, and her light red lipstick lit up her face when she smiled. For someone with a petite stature, she had a surprisingly strong voice, pronounced by a distinctive New York accent. I connected with her undeniable earnestness. She had a cool no-nonsense quality, yet she seemed friendly and trustworthy. If I didn't know that Katie was a high-powered business coach for an international consulting firm, I might have pegged her for an artist: the casual flare in her fashion style reminded me of confident creative types.

On September 19th, I spent an evening in a conference room grazing on hors d'oeuvres as I socialized with other entrepreneurs and business owners. At least fifty of us had gathered to hear Katie and her colleagues speak. In Katie's presentation, she promised that her unique coaching and training model would help us reach new heights in business. I was intrigued, but I didn't feel ready to commit to the year-long program when I left the event that night.

But on this eerie night in October, six weeks after the presentation, Katie showed up in my thoughts as a lifeline. In slippered feet and a white terrycloth bathrobe, I sat down at my desk and composed a short email message to her, attempting to cover my pain with professionalism:

> *Katie,*
>
> *It was lovely to connect with you again.*
>
> *I've been thinking about the [program] and its benefits. Are you available for a follow-up phone conversation? I have a few questions.*
>
> *Sincerely,*
>
> *Tonya Comer*

Without hesitation, I hit "send." A few hours later, Katie confirmed her availability for a 10:00 a.m. call on Tuesday.

Between hitting "send" and Tuesday morning, I managed to drop off my egg-stained car at the auto body shop to get it repainted. Much to my surprise, egg yolks damage the finish on paint. Not only had that Mischief Night prank taken an emotional toll on me; I also had to dig into my pocketbook to pay for it.

THE CONVERSATION

It was Tuesday. I was feeling anxious and the only thing that got me out of bed that morning was the thought of working out. Exercise was (and still is) my refuge and go-to for stress relief. My fitness routine would surely assuage my jangling case of nerves. It had to. It was only 7:00 a.m., but I could see that this day was going to require all the muscle I could muster. I put on black spandex leggings and the rest of my workout garb and headed for the gym on the lower level of my condo building.

Thirty minutes to go and back upstairs, I was getting anxious about the conversation with Katie. I finished my breakfast and began to prepare for the call. I found myself rearranging objects on the desk until I noticed my obsession. I shook my head, saying out loud, "Tonya, even amidst the messiness of your life, you seem to think this will make it feel tidy. Really?"

I chuckled at the absurdity of it.

Still in my spandex workout attire, I wrapped an off-white throw blanket over my shoulder as I tried to get comfortable on that chilly day in my home office of all-red brick walls. I wiggled myself around in my chair and took a sip from my mug of hot water and lemon. I took a deep breath and prepared myself for the call. Determined to stay grounded and focused, I scratched questions on a notepad to keep me in business mode: tell me about the program, the success of the program, expectations of the program . . . You get the picture, right? I didn't want to sound nervous or give away my "position" too readily. I wanted to appear poised, though I wasn't sure I would even be able to articulate a sentence.

So much was riding on this call. My starting point would be my business. Yes, if I could save the business then I could pull the rest of my life together. So I thought, anyway. *Should*

I tell her that I am undercharging for my services, as if to prove my worth to the world? How would it look to this high-powered professional that I am facing bankruptcy and on the verge of losing everything?

I felt ashamed, and I couldn't help wondering how she would see me if she knew I was failing myself, failing my business, failing . . .

Breathe, Tonya. Breathe.

The phone alarm chimed: 10:00 a.m. I called Katie. Through the speakerphone and in the best version of my business voice that my weakened emotional state would allow, I engaged in the usual pleasantries.

"Hi, Katie, how are you? . . . Did you have a nice weekend?"

When the moment seemed right, I created the context for the call. "I asked to speak with you because I would like to learn more about you and the coaching program. Can you share a little of your background?"

I was working from the script I'd created to interview Katie as if she were a candidate applying for a job. As any great coach would do, Katie turned the table to "interview" me. She asked about my experience, my goals, my dreams, my readiness to invest in a premium-priced and high-demand coaching program. She asked me what it would mean to me if I were to achieve my goals and, more importantly, what was blocking me from achieving them. In my fragile emotional state, I felt naked and exposed. I was embarrassed. In shock and dismay, I shook my head and thought, *How did I have the audacity to think I had anything together?*

With each question, I slouched down more. Soon, I was hunched over with my legs tucked into my chest in a seated fetal position, swaddled in the blanket around my shoulders. With tears rolling down my flushed cheeks, the words I choked out must have been almost incomprehensible. It reached the point where I'd had enough questioning and I begged Katie to take me on as a client. "Please, please, help me. I need help. I don't know what else to do. I don't know where else to go. If I fix my business, I can fix my life."

Nothing but silence on the other end of the speakerphone as I cried the ugly cry. I do not recall how long Katie was silent. Even though she said nothing, I knew that she was there. I did not feel alone.

When my crying became less intense, Katie spoke. "What has happened to you to have you experience such pain?"

Then an explosive moment. I confessed, "I had a meltdown in a parking lot after my car was egged by a group of mischievous young people. It all came crashing in on me. It was too much to bear, as I am experiencing my marriage falling apart, my business not doing well, my health deteriorating. I don't know what to do. I feel like a failure at everything. I even failed myself."

Locking my arms tighter around my shins, and tucking my chin between my knees, I folded deeper into my seated fetal position and sobbed. I could smell and taste my salty tears as they streamed down the sides of my nose, grazed my upper lip, and fell onto my sweaty spandex leggings, now wet with tears.

"I feel completely lost, alone . . . worthless," I said in a soft, child-like manner.

After a short silence, Katie replied, in a matter-of-fact and non-judgmental tone, "Let me tell you what I hear. Is that all right?"

"Yes," I replied, hesitantly.

"I hear a collapse of YOU and your circumstances. It's as if you ARE your circumstances. What do you think about what I am saying?"

With a jolt of astonishment, I raised my head and stared at the handset of the phone as if I were looking into Katie's eyes. "What do you mean?"

"You seem to think that your circumstances are you, and you are your circumstances."

I felt my eyebrows furrow, stunned by this revelation. The tears stopped. Silence. I pondered her statement. Though shocking, it was surprisingly comforting to hear her words.

"Tonya, you are not your circumstances," she continued. "I'd love to have you in my coaching program. But I recommend that you do some other transformational work beforehand. This work will allow you to separate WHO YOU ARE from your circumstances, so you are free to be and live your best life."

And that was the beginning of my journey to wholeness.

THE JOURNEY TO WHOLENESS

Katie revealed a blind spot to me. She could see something that I could not see in myself. And she was correct: I was unable to separate myself from my circumstances. I had been living in a state of victimhood, overwhelmed by pain and shame, and held back by self-doubt. And life's unpleasant events? Well, they all felt personal. Like when the eggs were painting my car in the convenience store parking lot, it felt like egg on MY face.

In 2009, I started a personal growth journey. Still, I remained stuck. My life on autopilot was taking me to the same places I had been before—until in 2011 when Katie's revelation redirected my course and set my transformational journey in motion. It was a gift that empowered me to bring consciousness to the journey of healing . . . and living. I would learn to see things for what they are, acknowledging my choices in the matters of the past, present, and future. I would take the steps to reconnect with my true self and embody a new way of living life—by my own design rather than by inauthentically pretending my way through life in the *mask du jour*.

Personal transformational work changed my life forever and birthed my passion for helping others with coaching and development. I have dedicated myself to the work of self-discovery—no matter where it might lead or what it might mean. After that breakthrough meeting with Katie, I took course after course and studied and practiced a wide range of modalities, methods, and distinctions that facilitated my personal growth and transformation.

Since 2011, I have put what I learned into practice in my life. It doesn't always work perfectly; I still falter. Some of the falls have been brutal. After all, I am human. In this life unexpected things are bound to happen. Thankfully, I am much better equipped to bounce back from the difficulties, challenges, and obstacles. This comes from healing emotional wounds by applying tools of transformation.

There was an a-ha moment in my journey. It inspired and emboldened me to write this book for you. While confronting painful memories from my past, I was suddenly overwhelmed by intense emotion. The pain was so unbearable that I cried out, "Why me?"

It was a question I would ask repeatedly for days. At last, I heard an answer from the voice of my intuition, *Tonya, your journey is not yours alone. You are to share it with others.*

In my shock, I tried to comprehend this message. A whisper followed, *Why NOT you?*

Empowered by that message, I am honored to share my lessons learned with you.

In taking on the assignment to write and publish this book, I dared myself to be the Katie in your life—the unapologetic champion of your wholeness. The circumstances and challenges you face in your life may look very different from the personal experiences I share throughout this book. What matters is that something important has stirred in you, called you to reach out for something more . . . inspired you to want the best for yourself and maybe even for others. And guess what? The flame inside of you is there for a reason. It is your truth begging to be revealed, begging to be lived. All you have to do is to know how to find it; and then, design a life in accordance with it. This book will guide you on a path to this truth and to living life by your own design.

CHAPTER ONE

Own It!

Are you aware of certain situations in your life that keep playing out over and over again? The circumstances may look something like this: You are repeatedly overlooked for a promotion, or you find yourself in romantic relationships where your partner cheats on you, or you frequently feel unheard by your partner or friend. It's like someone hit the replay button on the video screen of your life and you got stuck in an unhappy story.

In this chapter, we'll explore how the foundational beliefs you formed in childhood create negative patterns that play out endlessly in your life. Once you unmask the belief system behind these patterns, your life will begin to change dramatically.

Own It is the first of the 7 Power Tools for Designing Your Life. This tool gives you a process for learning how to identify your foundational belief and own the truth that it is rooted in story, not fact. This is liberating!

To illustrate the point of this chapter, I first want to share the childhood experiences that caused me to form a negative belief system, and then I'll show you how I got my power back by owning my experience. With the guidance I offer in the "Journey to Wholeness Design Space," you will learn how to rewrite your own story from a new perspective that empowers, rather than accepting the story as the truth and living life based on a big fat lie.

THE PROJECTS

To help me understand some things about her past and appease my curiosity about my past, my mother began to share stories with me when I was about seven years old. I could comprehend complex subjects at an early age, and she was aware of this fact. Thankfully, I have these stories to give context to critical aspects of my mom's life and their influence on mine.

At twenty-years-old, my mom sat alone on a park bench holding my tiny newborn body close and wondering what on earth to do. Moments of intimacy with a man had created this baby who was now fatherless and born into poverty. She had moved from homeless shelter to homeless shelter while growing up. And because of this, she knew that was no life for her baby. She wanted a better life for her child. So, she did the only thing she knew to do at the time. *Pray.* She sobbed and prayed. And she sobbed and prayed some more. When she began to question whether her prayers would be answered, she prayed again. It was a simple prayer: "Please help me. I need a miracle!"

It wasn't long before a perfect stranger, moved by my mom's tear-filled eyes and sheer desperation, came to her aid. This woman, whom I call "Angel," told my mom about the Housing Authority of the City of Pittsburgh (HACP), a government agency that placed low-income families in affordable housing.

Mama, a courageous fighter, soon found her way to the agency and requested housing assistance. The folks at HACP rallied in support of my mom and me by helping to find housing for us and identifying assistance programs for food, health care, and other services. The quick action of these folks made it possible for my mom to move us into a two-bedroom apartment in Arlington Heights, a hilltop government housing development project on the south side of the city.

Over the years, government housing developments around the country have become known in the urban vernacular as "The Projects." These neighborhood developments have been stereotyped as breeding grounds for crime, drugs, violence, gangs, and promiscuity, with indigent people living on welfare checks. The neighborhood where I grew up had some marijuana dealers and a few more who were users, a share of alcohol over-consumers, and an occasional narcotic incident, but it was not infested with abuse and crime. Most of the people in my predominantly Black community were respectable decent folks. Many of the adults made an honest living just like my mom, and they simply didn't earn enough income to support their families outside of this environment. Arlington Heights was a community, and quite a spirited and jovial one at that, with gregarious adults indulging in cardplaying shenanigans or dice-throwing games on the curbs of the street, and children riding their bikes or playing basketball at the nearby court. People were always looking out for each other, like when the "brothas" walking down the sidewalks would not hesitate to show some chivalry to the "sistas" who needed a hand carrying groceries or carting a baby and stroller off a bus. "The Projects" I grew up in cut against the grain of all those stereotypes.

For Mama and me, our little apartment on Arlington Avenue was home. Soon after moving into our apartment, Mama, in her thrifty and industrious fashion, created a home for us. She garnered hand-me-downs to fill our closets, found used furniture to fill the rooms, painted the walls, and hung ruffled cotton curtains on the windows. This little apartment, glowing from the bright yellow walls of the kitchen, became our home. Home had been a missing part of my mom's life since she was fourteen years old, when a family tragedy left her without a place to call home. On the day that Angel showed up in the park, it changed the trajectory of mom's life. To my mom, living in the Projects was progress, a step up in life. And for me, it was all I knew.

At some point in my early years, I traded playing with my Barbie doll for climbing trees with the boys. One time when I was being feisty, Mama humorously called me "Tony the Tiger." That very day, I declared my new nickname "Toni" (with an "i" not a "y"), and I forbid my family to call me *Tonya* ever again. Toni helped me to fit in with the boys in the "hood;" namely my closest friends Ricky and his older brother Romeo. Ricky, Romeo, and Toni. It just worked. Ricky, Romeo, and *Tonya?* Not the same effect.

By age eight, I was trusted to play in the nearby woods without supervision. I thoroughly enjoyed hightailing it through the concrete jungle of our neighborhood with Ricky and Romeo to play in the lush, wooded hills nearby.

We had a favorite tree—an evergreen standing probably thirty feet tall. Romeo would hoist me and Ricky to the lower branches and then we'd pull Romeo up. Then the three of us would navigate our way up the tree. At some point in the adventure, we'd all sit on the middle branches of the tree, with our hands and clothes sticky from sap, and talk about the silly things eight- and nine-year-old kids giggle about. When we weren't hanging out in the tree, we were out playing kickball or riding our bikes. This was how I preferred to spend my time—hanging with Ricky, Romeo, and the other boys who would join us from time to time.

THE CAFETERIA

From kindergarten to fifth grade, I attended Carmalt Elementary School, a magnet school offering specialized teaching programs to a diverse group of students from multiple school districts. The school's principles of inclusion and collaboration were innovative for the time. To foster its principles, the classrooms were set up in quads with no walls separating them. In first grade, I became fascinated by the vastness of the classroom quads. I loved the open space and the bold colors that delineated the different classrooms. This environment fed my creativity. So much so that today I credit the environment at this school for sparking my love for open-space floorplans as an interior designer.

I felt inspired at school. My teachers praised me for my creative spirit and commitment to my studies. I was eager to please my teachers, my mom, and my community. I preferred to sit in the front row in class, as I wanted to excel in school and instinctively thought this would help me do it. I loved interacting with the other students, and I fully participated in my classes.

I had strong social awareness and a sense of right and wrong. In school, I wanted everyone to be treated equally. I did my part by comforting the kids who were the outcasts and being friendly with the boisterous kids who demanded attention. I never felt the need to blend in, and I wasn't the type to demand being center stage. I wasn't the teacher's pet, nor was I the class clown. I had just a few friends and I liked it that way. When it came to settling arguments, I would rather hug than fight. I would seek to understand others rather than label them or call them names.

Despite my accepting nature, or maybe partly because of it, by the third grade, I had become a person to "pick on," as kids put it. I imagine some kids didn't know what to think of me. I must have been like a puzzle to them—unable to put it together—not only because of my inclusive attitude but also my ethnic ambiguity. As a fair-skinned, bi-racial girl with long, thin, curly dark-brown hair, light brown eyes, and facial features more European than stereotypically Black, I most certainly looked different from most kids.

Skin tone discrimination within the Black community has historical roots in slavery, when lighter-skinned Black folks had greater advantages than brown-skinned or dark-skinned people. Over a hundred and fifty years after the end of slavery, this cultural stigma has led to divisive and contentious relationships between light-skinned, brown–skinned, and dark-skinned Black folks. It still plays a role in the larger society, not just here in the United States, but also around the world.

In the third grade, I just wanted to blend in, as most kids do. I was unaware of the cultural and historical color-coded thinking and antagonism that existed in my own community. So, it was a shock to find myself the subject of a character attack by the popular Black girls in school. That was the moment when my world turned upside-down.

During lunch break, a group of nine-year-old girls, corralled by their ringleader Sarah, decided to make it known to me what they thought of me. Sarah yelled out from across the aisle at an adjacent cafeteria table, "Tonya is a goody two-shoes; she thinks she's all that."

Her posse joined her in a rhythmic high-pitched teasing voice, repeating: "Tonya is a goody two-shoes; she thinks she's all that."

All the girls in the clique laughed, and one of them belched out the words, "Tonya, you ain't all that."

Immediately, I dropped my head down, an instinctual response to the piercing pain I felt from the gut punch of their words and an attempt to hide myself from the penetrating gaze of the other students in the cafeteria. I studied the almond-colored lunch tray holding my lunch du jour of spaghetti with meat sauce, sliced pears in sugary syrup, a small red carton of milk with white letters, and a plastic cup of orange juice with the foil seal on top. Rather than tasting the food in my mouth, I was tasting salty tears.

The cafeteria usually felt bright and warm due to the pale-yellow cinder block walls, the fluorescent lighting, and the heat radiating from the commercial hot food stations which lined one side of the room. On this day, it felt like the coldest and loneliest place on earth. I felt such emptiness inside; it was a dark feeling of cold desperation . . . like trying to find a way out of an abyss of nothingness. And then, I had a thought: *I don't matter*. This feeling of loneliness and the thought that *I don't matter* would be etched in my memory as trauma. I felt isolated, humiliated, powerless, different—the perfect combination for shame. There would be no blending in with the other students now that I was publicly humiliated, and it was confirmed that I didn't belong.

The teasing didn't just end that day in the cafeteria. Sarah and her posse continued to harass me over the years. I was poked, prodded, and pushed. Perhaps they thought their physical provocation would beat "all that" out of me. Other kids started to show this cruel behavior toward me as well. Most of the time, I rose above it and walked away. Then, I'd find a place where I could be by myself and cry, usually in a bathroom stall or inside my locker with my foot wedged in the door to keep it from shutting. There was a time, though, when I couldn't take it anymore. So, I fought back.

THE BETRAYAL

In fifth grade, Ricky turned on me and became one of the instigators. A bus ride home from school one afternoon set a bitter conflict in motion between us, and that would be the last time I'd call Ricky my "friend."

It was a sunny day in late October, close to Halloween. I was wearing a light-pink and lime-green polka-dotted jacket, blue jeans, and a button-down yellow shirt. My plaited pigtails were held in place with pink hair ribbons and matching barrettes.

Ricky usually sat two seats behind me on the boarding side of the big yellow school bus. This day was no different. Ricky was usually a bit rambunctious and disruptive. This day was no different. Ricky would often pull my long hair and tease me by saying, "Tonya Comer. Tonya comb 'er hair too much."

The kids around us would laugh. This day was no different. You'd think it would get old, but nope.

There was one difference on this day. Ricky said words that I never thought I'd hear from a person I considered to be my friend. He said, "Lil' Miss Goody Two-Shoes, she must be adopted because she's white and her mom is black."

My fair skin tone does contrast with my mom's beautiful milk-chocolate brown complexion. Never once had I seen my skin as white. And it had never occurred to me that someone would call me "white."

Ricky continued, "Lil' Miss Goody Two-Shoes . . . she thinks she all that."

Those words went way beyond Ricky's usual jokes; they cut me like a knife, especially since they were uttered by a so-called friend. I wasn't quick witted enough to have a good comeback to his insulting remarks. So, I stood up in the bus and took two steps down the aisle toward him. I glared at him with the nastiest look, and said, in my fragile little girl voice, "You are so mean!"

Then, I balled up my hands into fists and slugged Ricky in the face with a right hook. Ricky pushed me. I lost my balance; he pushed me again. I pushed back. Then, Ricky punched me in the eye. The kids on the bus yelled, "Fight! Fight!"

During our brawl, the extremely agitated bus driver pulled the bus over to the side of the street and parked. Then he escorted me and my book bag to a seat at the front of the bus. My heart raced. My head throbbed. My hand ached. What hurt most was the humiliation.

It was the cafeteria moment being re-lived, but this time, with a person I called a friend. We reached the bus stop where many of the kids on the bus would exit, including Ricky and me.

When we exited the bus, Ricky pushed me again. I dropped my bag, and Ricky and I ended up in a full-out fight—throwing fists and tossing each other around on the sidewalk. Ricky was a few inches shorter than me with a stocky build, and his blows did not land softly. It was pure adrenaline and pent-up hurt that kept me fighting back. Eventually, one of my adult neighbors broke up this fight and escorted me home.

I never played with Ricky again. We sat far apart on the school bus for the rest of the school year. Of course, he tried to provoke me a few times, but I ignored him.

Once I had played comfortably in the middle between the cool kids and the less popular kids. But now, I had become a loner. I sat on the school bus in a row by myself. I traversed the halls of the school by myself. I climbed my favorite tree by myself. Alone. It had become my new familiar state.

For the two years that followed the cafeteria incident, I avoided lunch time; I resented spaghetti day; I hated the smell of the cafeteria; and when I got on my knees to pray every night, I begged God to let fifth grade come and go fast. I wanted to graduate to a new school to escape the daily reminders of the most humiliating day ever. The school, once my favorite place on earth, was just a daily reminder of what I wanted to hide from the most—*I don't matter*.

THE CULTURE

I was raised in a culture where the adults disciplined children by having them go out to a tree or bush to pick their own switch for a beating. If it was not feasible to get a branch for the beating, then the adult would deliver punishment using a broomstick, wood spatula, telephone cord, belt, hard-soled shoe, or any other object sure to cause enough pain to knock the "devil" out of the child. Parents and children often joked about this practice, even reveled in it as a code of conduct for parenthood.

The acceptance of this practice by the Black community seems twisted, given that it mirrors methods of punishment rooted in slavery. The master's beatings left the slaves feeling utterly dehumanized. Is it any wonder that mimicking this type of punishment by "whoopin" kids into submission and obedience might leave a child feeling devalued . . . even worthless? Unfortunately, I experienced this kind of punishment on one too many occasions, before I even started school. I was often beaten for no just cause. I began to internalize the feelings of being devalued and "less than" from an early age.

Studies in psychology would suggest that I may have begun to internalize these feelings of "less than" as early as in the womb, since my mom's intense feelings about being homeless and alone could have been transmitted to me. It's likely that feelings of "less than" began as a toddler while making observations about my world. Sitting in nursery school listening to the teacher read the story of Mama Bear, Papa Bear, and Baby Bear, processing everything in my little developing brain, I became aware that something was missing in my life. There was no Papa Bear.

In elementary school, I found a clear marker for my "different" identity by watching television shows and reading books that portrayed the traditional family structure. Where I grew up, I mostly saw single moms. Even more, I felt my mom's angst as a single mom and began to internalize her pain. I felt I was a daily reminder of the void in her life, especially since I must look more like my father than I do Mama. Why he was never in my life remains a mystery to me. But it's obvious that I was not conceived by two people who had a committed relationship. I internalized this fact and began to believe that I was conceived by mistake, and therefore, I was an "accident." I wasn't just dealing with a mommy wound and a daddy wound, longing desperately for the love of my two parents. I was living with an emptiness wound, longing desperately to feel like I mattered. This longing shaped the way I saw myself fitting in—or rather, *not* fitting in, to the world around me.

Before Sarah's cutting remark about me, I was already holding a secret belief that I was "less than." And I think the social chastisement I experienced in the cafeteria may have hurt me more than the belts and whips that once thrashed my little body, the guilt I felt as the source of mom's pain, and the emptiness I felt as an accident. It was a humiliating public exposure of my "less than" secret: *I don't matter.*

Add to that, the sharp sting of being harassed by my friend Ricky a few years later, and I formed the unshakable belief that I didn't matter to anyone, anywhere . . . not in my family, not at school, not to a friend. Loneliness and isolation became my bosom buddies, reinforcing the foundational belief—*I don't matter*.

I came to associate the feeling of being unaccepted or unwanted with *I don't matter.* Anytime this belief came up, I was instantly flooded with shame. It was like being transported right back to the cafeteria in third grade, tasting my salty tears and hanging my head as I studied the food on my lunch tray, feeling utterly alone.

It took decades for me to resolve the pain associated with those early experiences that had branded me with a false sense of myself as "less than" and to claim my new identity as a strong, empowered woman. I didn't suddenly see myself as "all that." That's not the way transformation works. I had to go through the healing process so that I no longer felt victimized by the events that set my foundational belief in motion. The first step was to own what happened and take responsibility for allowing myself to believe that I didn't matter. I had to *Own It.*

This first power tool in your transformational toolkit is a game changer—it gives you your power back. When you take ownership of your role in your life experiences, you don't let what happens in your life define or limit who you are. You let these moments teach you how to be all that you can be, all that you were meant to be.

Let's look at how your belief system may be the source of your shame and self-doubt. This awareness will help you to know the truth of who you really are . . . and you are true to yourself when you *Own It.*

POWER TOOL 1: OWN IT

We are "meaning-making" machines.

An event or experience that seems insignificant to one person may throw another person into a debilitating funk or an emotional uproar. Why is this so? As a human, you're conditioned to assign meaning to things. It's inherent to your survival in this world. You constantly make decisions and judgments in response to your environment. The meanings you assign to an event will depend on how you perceive and interpret it. That's why two people can be at the same place at the same time and have a completely different experience. The meanings you assign to things can be positive, good, favorable, affirming; or they can be negative, harmful, unfavorable, destructive. It's important for you to become aware of the meanings you assign to events. Your negative perceptions can interfere with living a fully expressed, abundant life, filled with acceptance and love.

All the events in your life have one thing in common. Simply put, they happen. It doesn't matter whether the event was planned, predictable, or by accident. The event—the "it"—just happened.

> In and of themselves, the things that happen in your life have no meaning. It's your response to these events and the stories you project onto them that give them their meaning.

Let's take the simple example of a weather event to help you understand how you may project meaning onto things. To you, the rain may be a welcome event: "Yay, it's raining! Now, I don't have to water my lawn."

Whereas to your neighbor, rain may not be welcome. "Bummer. It's always gloomy and miserable when it rains."

Do you see how the rain can have a completely different meaning to two people depending on their perspective? Neither point of view is right or wrong, good or bad. The meaning someone projects on the rain doesn't impact the rain at all. The rain is neutral. It is just rain. This holds true for all the experiences you have in life, even the most painful ones. The event, in and of itself, has no meaning. You give it one.

It's not easy to see how you project meaning onto things, because you do it so automatically that you're not usually aware you're doing it. Let's look at an example of how this dynamic plays out in an event that could have happened in your early development. Imagine that the "it" for you is *dad missed my piano recital.*

Dad missed your piano recital. That's what happened. It doesn't mean that your dad doesn't love you. It doesn't mean that he likes your brother more than he likes you. It doesn't mean that his work is more important to him than you. Whatever you conclude is a meaning you attached to the event. The event itself—the "it"—didn't decide that for you. Of course, this experience could produce myriad emotions in you, especially negative ones difficult to manage as a child. But the meaning you give this experience is your own decision.

Maybe for you it wasn't your piano recital, maybe it was your soccer game, or dance recital, or school play, or science exhibition, or birthday party. And maybe it wasn't your dad. It was your mom, or auntie, or sibling, or favorite teacher. My point here is to show how you attach meaning to the experiences in your life based on how you perceive and identify with an event. Then you allow the event to impact how you feel about yourself and how you define yourself. What happened is not *who you are*.

We often believe that what happens to us also defines us.

A lot of who you believe "you are" is not the essential truth of who you are. Your belief system works to convince you otherwise.

Word creates world. The words you say out loud or to yourself shape your reality. They shape what you see, hear, expect, do, and believe. Negative beliefs are formed because of the words you have spoken about yourself—or others have spoken about you—that you've convinced yourself are true. It's true because of the natural impulse to give meanings to words (and other things) and build a belief system around them.

Let's take a closer look at how this belief system works. Negative beliefs are known under the common umbrella term, self-limiting (or limiting) beliefs. It's helpful to examine the four aspects of self-limiting beliefs and how they impact you.

Self-Worth Beliefs

Deep down, you may have a belief that "I am not good enough." This is one of three *self-worth beliefs*. These beliefs cause you to feel you don't deserve this or that, and these beliefs arise from the idea that you are without something or lacking something. Therefore, you are not enough of something. The three beliefs about self-worth are: "I am not good enough," "I am not worthy," and "I am not deserving."

Foundational Beliefs

You have a fundamental need to belong; it's part of your humanity. If you feel that you are somehow flawed, then you question your ability to be accepted by others and to secure a sense of belonging in the world around you.

A *foundational belief* is rooted in the need for belonging. These beliefs are core beliefs deeply rooted in your identity and surface because of meanings you assigned to yourself during impactful events and experiences in your life. There are typically three or four critical moments in your life—in early childhood, at puberty, and in early adulthood—in which you define who you are. Positive experiences can define you at these ages. It is true though that, for many, the more challenging moments in your early life (from birth to seven years old) will be a heavy anchor for your identity.

Common events might include:

- when parents get divorced

- when there is domestic violence involving parents or others

- when one is scolded as a child

- when one is criticized, ridiculed, or bullied

- when a parent misses an important event

- when one is having trouble with learning or reading

- when one struggles in an activity or sport

- when one loses a loved one or friend to death

- when a loved one or friend moves away

- when the girl/boy one likes does not respond in kind

- when physical or sexual abuse occurs

- when heartbreak occurs with a crush or love relationship

- when there is prolonged exposure to stressful and uncontrollable events

A challenging and emotionally charged experience such as one of these described above may have greatly impacted you as a child. It may have shaped the construction of your identity, especially as you would compare yourself to the world around you. Often in a moment of reckoning the event and what you think it means about you as a person, you form a foundational belief.

> Your foundational belief is like an anchor holding you in place; it feels impossible to change—like an undeniable, unrelenting truth. And you then hold on to this belief like you're serving a life sentence—a form of punishment for a crime for which you have been found guilty.

We all have at least one—but no more than two—foundational beliefs.

Common foundational beliefs are:

- *I am not lovable*

- *I don't matter*

- *I am unwanted*

- *I am invisible*

- *I am bad*

- *I am too much*

- *I am powerless*

- *I am a failure (a loser)*

- *I am never enough*

Do you identify with any of these? If it is not apparent, you will have an opportunity to do some discovery work in the "Journey to Wholeness Design Space" at the end of the chapter; and throughout the book, you may have more revelations about your foundational belief. Let's continue. There's more to it.

Circumstantial Beliefs

Your *circumstantial beliefs* serve as physical, tangible, or identifiable "evidence" to validate the truth of your foundational beliefs. In other words, you let circumstances justify your foundational belief. Therefore, circumstantial beliefs are only true in your perception and perspective. And they are often changeable, conditional, and/or consequential.

To your belief system, the circumstantial nature of the evidence makes no difference. So, if the circumstance—or evidence—goes away, you will still hold the foundational belief as true. And sometimes, you convince yourself that the circumstantial belief is still true even when it ceases to be true in reality.

Some examples of circumstantial beliefs are:

- *I am (too) fat*
- *I am (too) thin*
- *I am not smart*
- *I am alone*
- *I am not pretty*
- *I am too young*
- *I am not popular*

Let's examine how foundational beliefs and circumstantial beliefs relate to each other.

Let's assume your foundational belief is *I am not lovable.* You might hold a circumstantial belief "I am fat" as a justification for why you are not lovable. For you, "I am fat" is a circumstantial belief; it is evidence for why you KNOW without argument that you are not lovable. Notice, though, that "I am fat" is only a perception and is a condition that can change.

Let's assume your foundational belief is *I am unwanted,* and you hold a circumstantial belief "I am alone." For you, you 'know'—and nothing can convince you otherwise—that you are unwanted because you are alone. Do you see that "I am alone" is a perspective and is consequential? It can happen because of some other condition or as a consequence of some other thing that may have occurred.

Let's assume your foundational belief is *I am invisible.* If your circumstantial belief is "I am not popular," you have evidence that you are invisible because you are unpopular. And you may argue—mostly with yourself—until you are blue in the face to prove that you are invisible because of this evidence. Can you see that "I am not popular" is a perspective that is conditional and changeable?

No matter what self-limiting beliefs you hold, let me assure you: None of these beliefs are the truth of who you are.

> You live in a fabricated reality with a negative self-image and a false identity, believing these things to be your truth. The real truth is that you made it all up.

These false perceptions were merely an interpretation of your experience—the meaning you assigned to an event. That's all. You made the event mean something about you. The meaning you assigned is not your truth. Yet, this false reality dictates the stories you tell yourself (and maybe others) about who you are, who you aren't, why you do what you do, why you don't do what you don't do, what you fear, and why you feel unworthy and inherently flawed.

Impostor Beliefs

You hold your self-limiting beliefs (self-worth beliefs, foundational beliefs, and circumstantial beliefs) inside, and you try to protect them from being exposed. You do everything you can to keep the beliefs safe, as a secret between you and yourself. You present one face to the world; but inside, you hold a very different view of yourself. Because of this, you believe "I am a fraud" or "I am an impostor." The experience associated with *impostor beliefs* is known commonly as the "Impostor Syndrome."

You fear that your secret will be found out or your mask will fall. You fear that if the world finds out that you are not who you present yourself to be, you will be condemned, scarred publicly for your lie AND for your so-called truth. It feels like a no-win situation. And this fear can be overwhelming, debilitating even.

Self-worth beliefs, foundational beliefs, circumstantial beliefs, and impostor beliefs are four aspects of your self-limiting belief system. They form because of the meanings you assign to words spoken to, through, and about you, as well as the meanings you assign to the events and conditions of your life. These beliefs, anchored by the foundational belief, build on themselves and reinforce each other. It's a repetitive pattern which has a detrimental impact on how you see yourself and how you view the events and experiences in the past, present, and future aspects of your life.

We find ourselves in a vicious cycle.

vicious cycle (noun):

a sequence of reciprocal cause and effect in which two or more elements intensify and aggravate each other, leading inexorably to a worsening of the situation.[1]

Of your self-limiting beliefs, the foundational belief is the anchor. It distorts your reality and causes you to manifest that false reality by attracting more experiences to affirm its truth over and over again. The meanings that you assign to an event or thing influence how you feel about it. How you feel influences the behavior in the moment, which, in turn influences the outcomes that you get. The outcomes reinforce the meaning that you created. That cycle continues again. The meanings that you assign to an event or thing influence how you feel about it . . . and so on.

Let's refer to our example: *Dad missed your piano recital.* Remember, the piano recital could be another event like your soccer game, or dance recital, or school play, or science exhibition, or birthday party. Let's say that after Dad missed your event, you felt abandoned. So, you made it mean that *I am unwanted.* As you have convinced yourself that you are unwanted, that you will be left or abandoned for being unwanted, you see other events in your life through the same filter of being unwanted. So, when the boyfriend breaks up with you, you think, *I am unwanted*. When you aren't selected as a member of the orchestra, you think *I am unwanted*. When your best friend forgets to call you on your birthday, you think *I am unwanted*. You begin to see life through the filter of your foundational belief.

Have you ever purchased a new car, and then suddenly, you notice other cars just like yours all around you—on the road, in the parking lot, on television? You didn't notice these cars before you purchased your own, it's as if they just show up suddenly. Well, they just didn't show up out of nowhere. They've been there all along. It's because, in simplest terms, the reticular activation system (RAS) in your brain filters through all the information it takes in and finds the familiar. So, you begin to see the similar cars because your brain has a reason to filter all cars to focus on what is familiar.

The RAS supports your foundational belief by looking for all the evidence that supports the belief. It filters information and finds that which is like the original trigger . . . be it the smells, sounds, physical characteristics, moods, attitudes, anything that resembles the original event—the original trauma. It draws on familiarity. And when it does, you begin to feel the same way you felt during the original event. You end up in a vicious cycle of sameness . . . playing out the same old self-sabotaging patterns without realizing why it is happening.

Our practices are a manifestation of our beliefs.

You live in a world in which you are your own creation. You may become what you desire. Unbeknownst to you, your foundational belief operates as a barometer by which you define yourself and who you become. And, as shocking as it is to accept and maybe even to comprehend, you become the person you say you least want to be.

You become the *I am not lovable* person waiting to not be loved. You become the *I don't matter* person waiting to feel unimportant. You become the *I am unwanted* one waiting to be abandoned. You become the *I am invisible* being waiting to be unheard or unseen. You become the *I am bad* person waiting to be bad. You may become the *I am too much* woman waiting to be too much. You become the *I am powerless* person waiting to be weak. You become the *I am a failure (a loser)* one waiting to miss the mark or fall short in some way. You become the *I am never enough* person waiting to never be enough. How do you know that this is so? You demonstrate self-sabotaging behaviors.

If your foundational belief is *I am not lovable:*

You may sabotage any act of love that you or others try to demonstrate. You may become promiscuous or non-committal. You may become a recluse, you may be aloof. You may avoid intimacy and close relationships. You may push people away emotionally. You may be easily manipulated or taken advantage of in relationships. You may have issues with trust in relationships—romantic and otherwise. Why? You may hold the belief that he/she/they don't love you. You may also have opposite practices: you may go out of your way to prove that you are lovable, only to sabotage it by rejecting another's love. It isn't that you want to reject love. With the beliefs you hold and the practices you've developed, you simply know no other way.

If your foundational belief is *I don't matter:*

You may sabotage any opportunity to feel important. You may become a loner, you may find yourself experiencing abusive or neglectful situations, you may shy away from the limelight or the stage, you may acquiesce to others' needs and desires and downplay your own. Why? You may hold the belief that people do not value you. You may also have opposite practices: you may go out of your way to prove that you matter by becoming a people pleaser or overly charitable, only to sabotage it by complaining that you always give and everyone takes from you. It isn't that you want to reject the feeling of mattering. With the beliefs you hold and the practices you've developed, you simply know no other way.

If your foundational belief is *I am unwanted:*

You may sabotage any opportunity to feel wanted. You may find that your pattern is to be a loner. You may avoid getting too close to others. You may be less likely to develop long-term relationships. You may have a hard time keeping friendships. You may avoid intimacy or push people away emotionally. You may create an island around you and convince yourself that it is better to be alone than to be left alone. You may have difficulty with trusting yourself and others in romantic relationships and other types of relationships, too. Why? You may hold the belief that no matter what you do, she/he/they will leave you . . . abandon you. You may also have opposite practices: you learn to charm and be likable to prove that you are wanted and desirable. Then, you sabotage it by doing the things that cause someone to leave you. It isn't that you want to reject someone who wants you; it is simply that with the beliefs you hold and the practices you've developed, you know no other way.

If your foundational belief is *I am invisible:*

You may sabotage any opportunity to be seen or heard. You may find that your pattern is to be shy and timid, you may become a loner, you may avoid intimacy or push people away emotionally. You may be a nomad. You may avoid speaking unless being spoken to or unless it is essential. Why? You may hold the belief that no matter what you do, she/he/they will not see you or hear you. So, you tiptoe around and avoid making noise and creating a spectacle of yourself. You may also have opposite practices: You may be overly loud and outspoken (as to be heard) or be overly demonstrative (as to be seen). Then, you sabotage it by doing things which cause someone to not see you or hear you. It isn't that you want to reject someone who wants to see or hear you; it is simply that with the beliefs you hold and the practices you've developed, you know no other way.

If your foundational belief is *I am bad:*

You may sabotage any opportunity to be seen as a good person or even-tempered. You may be gregarious, have grandiose plans and exaggerated emotions, and get into brawls easily or make enemies quickly. You may engage in manipulative, intimidating, harmful, or impulsive behaviors. You may demonstrate traits of entitlement and self-centeredness; it may appear that you focus on your own interest at the expense of others' happiness and well-being. You may also have an overall negative outlook on life which impacts your interactions with other people. Why? You may hold the belief that no matter what you do, she/he/they will think you are bad. You may also have opposite practices: You may find yourself holding back your feelings or expression, you may hold a sunken posture, you may avoid positions of leadership or authority. You may sabotage these overcompensating behaviors by doing something that causes you to be seen as bad. It isn't that you want people to not like your character; it is simply that with the beliefs you hold and the practices you've developed, you know no other way.

If your foundational belief is *I am too much:*

You may sabotage any opportunity to be seen as just enough. You may demand attention and seek to get it by almost any means necessary. You may seek the limelight, the center stage. You may be overly eager to engage with people or things. You may have grandiose ideas and exaggerated emotions. You may appear to focus on your own interest at the expense of others' happiness and well-being. Why? You may hold the belief that no matter what you do, she/he/they will think you are too much. You may also have opposite practices: You may find yourself holding back your feelings or expression, you may hold a sunken posture, you may avoid interactions with people. You may sabotage these overcompensating behaviors by doing something that causes you to be seen as too much. It isn't that you want people to not like your character; it is simply that with the beliefs you hold and the practices you've developed, you know no other way.

If your foundational belief is *I am powerless:*

You may sabotage any act of bravery and courage that would have you experience your own strength. You may become shy and timid and indecisive. You may become abnormally overwhelmed in stressful situations or when things change. You may be easily confused and disoriented. You may be overly dependent on others, especially those with authority. You may fault others for your unpleasant experiences and reactions, i.e., "they made me do it." Why? You may hold the belief that he/she/they will dominate or exercise their power, authority, or will over you. You may also have opposite practices: you may seek to manipulate, dominate, or control people or things. You may also become easy to anger and charge, or be easily defensive. It isn't that you want to reject your own bravery, courage, and strength, it is that you simply know no other way because of the beliefs you hold and the practices you've developed.

If your foundational belief is *I am a failure (loser):*

You may sabotage any opportunity to experience yourself as winning or being victorious over something. You may have a low tolerance and impatience when working on tasks. And when you try new things, you may give up easily if it doesn't work out or if it seems difficult. You may become abnormally overwhelmed in stressful situations. You may find it easier to quit a job, relationship, or opportunity than to ride out a wave. So, you may languish at the bottom of a career path, or the dating pool, or the housing ladder, or the adventure scale. Why? You may hold the belief that you always fail or always lose. You may also have opposite practices: You may push to excel and be the best only to set the bar so high that it is out of reach, and you sabotage your feeling of being successful or a winner when you fall short of the target. It isn't that you want to reject your feeling of being a success and a winner, it is that you simply know no other way because of the beliefs you hold and the practices you've developed.

If your foundational belief is *I am never enough:*

You may sabotage any opportunity to feel like you are enough. You may start things and never finish them. You may keep yourself from getting too close to others. You may avoid intimacy or push people away emotionally. You may be a recluse or limit your interactions with people to superficial engagement or to only when you deem it necessary. You may avoid positions of authority or leadership. You may sit in the corner or at the back of the room at a social event to avoid the limelight and/or the intimacy of others. Why? You may hold the belief that no matter what you do, you will never be enough for him/her/them. You may also have opposite practices: You may demand control of things. You may be an overachiever, demanding perfection of everything (you, others, things.) You do this to prove that you are enough. Here's the sabotage: Because the unrealistic expectations will naturally reveal imperfections, this causes you and others to question your "enough-ness." It isn't that you want to reject someone who accepts you as you are; it is simply that with the beliefs you hold and the practices you've developed, you know no other way.

To keep the story alive that the foundational belief is true, you also develop another interesting pattern. You change the statement to a question. This question becomes another form of sabotage.

We ask the unanswerable question.

You hold the foundational belief as a statement of fact and as a question. We may ask the question verbally. Often, though, the questions are not asked verbally but expressed implicitly through the validation we seek from others and the behaviors we demonstrate.

- If we believe *I am not lovable*, then the question we would ask or seek to validate is: "Do you love me?"

- If we believe *I don't matter*, then the question we would ask or seek to validate is: "Do I matter to you?"

- If we believe *I am unwanted,* then the question we would ask or seek to validate is: "Will you leave me?"

- If we believe *I am invisible,* then the question we would ask or seek to validate is: "Do you see me?" Or "Do you hear me?"

- If we believe *I am bad,* then the question we would ask or seek to validate is: "Am I a bad person?"

- If we believe *I am too much,* then the question we would ask or seek to validate is: "Am I too much for you?"

- If we believe *I am powerless,* then the question we would ask or seek to validate is: "Am I powerful (strong) enough for you?"

- If we believe *I am a failure (a loser),* then the question we would ask or seek to validate is: "Am I successful enough for you?" Or "Am I a winner to you?"

- If we believe *I am never enough,* then the question we would ask or seek to validate is: "Am I enough for you?"

These questions lead to the ultimate self-sabotage. There can be no satisfactory or acceptable answer to these questions. How can you affirm the opposite of what you have already convinced yourself is the truth? You cannot accept an answer to contradict the belief. You will reject the answer. This means then that the question you are asking is unanswerable to you.

Let's assume your belief is *I am unwanted.* No matter how many times you ask me "Will you leave me?" and I affirm that I will NOT leave you, you will not believe me. Why? It is the nature of your belief system to protect yourself. To do so, it keeps manifesting situations that reinforce the belief, and it rejects anything that contradicts it. Your belief system will not accept my opposing perspective as the truth. Its truth is the belief system it holds. This means that it's impossible for me—or anyone for that matter—to answer this question in a way that would satisfy you. In other words, the question is unanswerable; not because it couldn't be answered, but because it is unanswerable to you. You will reject the answer.

So, you have these self-limiting beliefs. They are anchored by the foundational belief. The foundational belief causes a vicious cycle, which is a form of sabotage. The masterful foundational belief converts itself into a question—an unanswerable one at that—which becomes then another form of sabotage. So, now what?

Now, we own it.

To *Own It* is to identify and take responsibility for the meaning you have created about yourself and your life. Own the fact that you have created this belief system about yourself. No one has forced you to hold these beliefs.

When you do this, you can detach yourself from the emotion of the initial event and you will realize that you do not have to hold yourself responsible for, or defined by, what happened. And you no longer feel the need to hold yourself captive to the meaning and the story. Why? Because it was all made up . . . and by you. Go figure.

Even though Sarah told me that "I ain't all that," it didn't make her statement true. I was the one who convinced myself it was true. Even though Sarah and the other kids in school teased, ridiculed, and bullied me, their actions did not confirm the truth of the statement. I was the one who determined that it was true and made the decision that *I don't matter.* And the events which laid the groundwork for that belief—the abuse as a child, internalizing mom's pain, and feeling like an accident—in which I held feelings of "less than" were just events. I made up that I was "less than."

In owning this, I gave myself permission and freedom to be anything I want—even someone who matters. I invite you to give yourself permission to be anything that you want to be, too.

JOURNEY TO WHOLENESS DESIGN WORKSPACE: OWN IT

DISCOVERY & PRACTICE

Grab your *The 7 Power Tools for Designing Your Life Journal* or notebook and a pen or pencil.

This is your time.

Choose a quiet, sacred place for this reflection where you can be undisturbed and where you feel free, comfortable, safe, and unencumbered by distractions. Find a seated position in which you feel most comfortable, either on a floor cushion or sitting on a sofa or chair. Have lots of drinking water and a box of tissues nearby. Feel free to light fragrance-free candles and dim the lights. Avoid stimulating your senses with visual information, music, incense, alcohol, cigarettes, or any potential distractions. The point is to drop into the space of reflection.

Please note that some traumatic memories may require the support of a therapist or counselor. Trust yourself. If you experience an abnormal level of fear or anxiety on this journey and question "going there" because it may be too traumatic, then consult a therapist and request support in completing this process. It's okay. Your healing is worth it, and so are you.

Take a deep breath, and let's start the *Own It* Process.

Take this time to reflect on your earliest memory of a defining event in your life. In your journal, respond to the following questions:

- What was the event?

- Who was there?

- What was the environment like?

- What did you hear?

- What did you see?

- What was said?

- What did you not say that you wish you had said at that time?

- What did you make it all mean about you?

Next, refer to the list below of the common foundational beliefs. Determine which of them fits you and your situation. If a belief comes up that's not on the list, write that down as well. If you stop at "I am not good enough," I encourage you to dig deeper. Remember, I am not good enough is a belief of self-worth, not a foundational belief. Pay attention to the complaints you have when you are upset with a friend or partner, when you feel your lowest, when you want things to go some way other than the way they are going, and when you talk about what's missing in your life. These complaints are good indicators of the beliefs you hold. You will know that you've identified your foundational belief when it causes a visceral reaction. The most common foundational beliefs are:

- *I am not lovable*

- *I don't matter*

- *I am unwanted (I am going to be left or abandoned)*

- *I am invisible (I am not seen or heard)*

- *I am bad*

- *I am too much*

- *I am powerless*

- *I am a failure (I am a loser)*

- *I am never enough*

Take this time to look for your patterns of thought and behavior relative to this foundational belief.

- What is the vicious cycle in your life?

- How does it play out?

- What is its impact on you and your life?

Write it all down. And be with it. Allow whatever feelings and emotions it triggers to come up. Don't resist feelings or emotions, don't run from them, don't justify them, don't blame them, don't repress them. Be with them.

Remember, "it" just happened. It's not who you are. "It" doesn't define you.

Now, *Own It.*

Own that you gave the event the meaning.

Own that you were in control of the interpretation.

Own that the foundational belief is rooted in story.

Own that it is not fact.

Own that you created the story.

Breathe.

Rinse and repeat. (Rinse by drinking water. Repeat the process.)

NOTE: You will find these instructions "Rinse and repeat" in many of the "Journey to Wholeness Design Workspace" sections at the end of each chapter. Rinse and repeat is an important part of the process in our journey to wholeness.

As a common instruction on your shampoo bottle, "rinse and repeat" encourages repeat cleansing until the hair is squeaky clean. Similarly, in your wholeness journey, you are in a practice of cleansing until you find no more residue. So, rinse by drinking water and repeat until you feel you've developed the awareness or met the objective of the assignment. Do so until there is no more residue. It's then that we can move on to the next chapter.

In the *Own It* practice, rinse and repeat encourages you to repeat the steps with multiple events in your life. This will allow you to witness how your foundational belief was shaped and understand the impact of its cycle of reinforcement and validation on you and your life.

CHAPTER TWO

Choose It!

When you look back on your life and make an honest assessment of the worst experiences you've lived through, no matter how traumatic, strange, inconceivable, challenging, or dark, can you see any good that has come with or because of these experiences? Perhaps they helped you to build strength and courage to face new challenges or taught you something important about yourself that led to making better choices. It's not easy to see the "seed of good" in a difficult experience when it's happening, but the wisdom and power you get as a result is extraordinarily beneficial. And on this journey to wholeness, the practice of choosing your perspective to reframe things and find the seed of good is a critical step to living an empowered life.

Perhaps you're thinking, "I wish I didn't have to go through negative experiences to get this 'good seed.'"

Of course, we all have had those thoughts. Still though, would your life be fulfilling if you didn't encounter experiences that challenge you to learn and grow? It is quite possible that it would not be. Perhaps life by its very nature is only worthwhile because of its experiences—be they deemed favorable or not. Perhaps humanity is made stronger as a whole because of the lessons we learn in life by finding courage after a fall, by finding resolution after conflict, by having success after repeated failure.

As you discovered with Power Tool 1: *Own It,* you are free to choose the meaning you assign to an event. With awareness and practice, you will see that you can quickly shift the meanings you assign to anything. Taking ownership of your experiences is the first step toward the shift.

In this chapter, we further explore the power of choice with Power Tool 2: *Choose It.* If you are willing to see a situation for what it is and recognize the freedom to choose your response, life will reward you. By becoming aware of your thoughts and being willing to own that some thoughts serve you better than others, you tap into your power—the power to choose your thoughts; the power to choose your reactions; the power to choose a life that empowers, enriches, and elevates you.

For decades, I carried lingering wounds of feeling objectified and violated. It wasn't until I understood the power of choice that I broke free from the cage of victimhood, healed the wounds, and rose up stronger than I had ever known myself to be.

THE LEMON

It was 1991, and I was a sophomore at one of my hometown's fine collegiate institutions, Duquesne University. I was thrilled to have just purchased my first car, a 1984 Volkswagen Jetta GL Turbo, 5-speed manual transmission, white with a black interior. The car was in good condition if you overlooked the fact that it had a faulty transmission. With my $2,000 budget, I could afford to buy the lemon and "turn it into lemonade." Well, at least that's what my then-boyfriend Kai believed was possible.

Despite his initial confidence and enthusiasm, repairing the car would turn out to be a bigger challenge than Kai, the self-proclaimed mechanic, anticipated. Kai had a strong desire to take care of "home base." Because I was his home base, he took pride in looking out for me and my needs. He had traditional values, and he fulfilled his boyfriend role in a respectful and respectable manner. Always a gentleman, always inclusive, always supportive. I was equally respectful and supportive of him. We had a healthy co-created partnership.

When it came to fixing the lemon, take-care-of-home-base Kai deeply desired to send me out on the road in a safe car that would drive as good as new. For months, his efforts to repair the Jetta were to no avail. It sat in disrepair in the driveway at his grandparents' home.

In the meantime, Kai allowed me to drive one of his two cars—a red 1984 Pontiac Fiero Coupe two-seater. I loved driving the Fiero. It was a good-looking car, and I felt good in it. As it turned out, though, the car was unreliable. With its temperamental radiator and engine design, the all-too-cute Fiero was frequently hoisted onto the bed of a tow truck and transported to some repair shop or to Kai's workshop in the driveway of his grandparents' home. Not having a reliable car complicated my travels, especially to work.

THE JOBS

It was hard for a girl from the Projects to pay rent, tuition, and buy books while attending an expensive liberal arts university. So, I worked several jobs. I found positions at the local radio conglomerate downtown, about a mile from the university. At American Urban Radio Networks (AURN), I worked as an audio journalist for the Saturday morning national news. For WAMO, I worked with my mentor Tené Croom, the legendary national news radio show host, as the co-producer of a radio show giving teenagers a voice on current events and news that impacted their world and their communities. On Sunday mornings, I was an audio engineer for WJZZ, where I hosted the gospel radio shift. And occasionally, I got to be on open mic as a disc jockey for the jazz radio segments.

A few nights a week, I worked for an invention company just a few blocks away from the radio networks as a research coordinator responsible for editing copy and verifying data for patent applications.

And I'd recently traded in a job at Kaufmann department store for a paid internship at a market research company in Bethel Park. It was about a thirty-five-minute commute by car. By public transportation, it was about an hour and a half commitment, as it involved taking two buses and walking about thirty minutes. Thus, the pressing need to purchase the Jetta.

THE BEST FRIEND

At times when the Fiero croaked, I occasionally had the great privilege of having my best friend Sanjay as my personal chauffeur.

Somehow, in the homogeneous city of Pittsburgh, I managed to become friends with the only Mumbai-native boy in the public school system. This may not be true, but it certainly seemed so from our perspectives. Sanjay and I met at an event as juniors in high school. I was one of the student lecturers at a Project LEAD event held at Soldiers and Sailors Memorial Hall, an event space and museum built to honor the U.S. branches of military and public service.

Project LEAD was designed for student leaders to guide conversations about subjects that mattered to their peers. On the day I met Sanjay, I was leading the conversation about safe sex. Sanjay and my cousin Danny were participants.

After the event, Danny, proud to see me in action, hugged me tightly. Then, he introduced me to Sanjay. We agreed to get together the following weekend and have dinner with their friends Jordan and Jay. The rest, as they say, is history. Their quartet became a quintet. Although I lived a river and a bridge away from them and we went to different high schools, somehow, I became part of this guy group, just as I had with Ricky and Romeo a decade earlier.

Over time, Sanjay and I grew very close, and to this day I still consider him my best friend. We're like two peas in a pod. We both love adventure, experiencing life to its fullest, are humanitarians, are generous and kind, are accepting and open-minded, thrive socially because we love people, and adore travel. He's my brother from another mother. Having him in my life is one of my life's greatest blessings.

Being my chauffeur back in college was a role Sanjay enjoyed, especially because it satisfied his overprotective nature, always wanting to ensure my safety and happiness.

THE BUS

One day when the Fiero needed repair and Sanjay was working, I had to rely on public transportation to get to and from school and work. When I was growing up, public transportation was the only way I knew to get around until my mother got her first car in my senior year of high school. So, commuting by bus was never an issue for me. On this day, though, when I took the #71A bus from Oakland to my job downtown, I had one of the most traumatic experiences of my life.

It was a beautiful sunny afternoon in early summer. One of the nice things about riding the bus was being part of the shared experience with the other passengers. When the weather was sunny and warm, the energy on the bus was generally lively and happy. But on this day, it was unusually quiet. The passengers boarded, chose their seats, and rode in silence.

I sat with an upright posture on the slightly worn, light-blue vinyl upholstered seat three rows from the front of the bus on the boarding side. Across from me was a young rider, perhaps in her early teens, bobbing her head to the tunes playing through the headphones of her Walkman radio. The bus driver, a heavy-set Black man dressed in a light blue Port Authority uniform, probably in his mid-forties, seemed to be in his own world and on autopilot as passengers boarded and got off the bus at each stop.

As the bus was approaching my stop at Sixth Avenue and Smithfield Street, I stood up and walked to the front. After the bus driver had stopped and pulled the manual arm to open the door, I acknowledged him, as I would typically, "Thank you, sir. Have a very nice day."

With his right hand, he aggressively reached for my left arm and pulled me closer to him. Then he quickly released my arm, reached for my butt, and palmed and fondled it. Slapping it affectionally, he said, "You have a nice day, too."

I looked at him in shock. I opened my mouth to speak. No words came out. Nothing. Only silence. I turned back to look at the few people on the bus, hoping for someone, anyone, to be my voice—to speak for me. I caught the eye of one woman, but she said nothing. Nothing. My heart raced. A tear fell from my right eye. The seconds felt like minutes as I looked at the passengers, desperate for help, for connection, for someone to be my voice. No one spoke up for me.

Could it be that someone saw the incident and didn't care enough to help me? Was I not important enough to be helped . . . supported . . . acknowledged?

I got off the bus as quickly as I could. I looked at the three people who were waiting there at the bus stop.

Could it be that one of them saw what happened and didn't care to help me?

I turned back and looked at the driver, who was staring straight ahead as he closed the door and drove off.

Could it be that this was just a regular day in his work shift, and I was just another casual victim of his unsolicited groping?

I began to feel faint. I dragged my limp body toward the office building at the corner. I leaned my back against the concrete wall to support myself, and perhaps even subconsciously trying to hide the filth that marred the backside of my two-piece peach skirt suit. I stood there frozen, unable to speak, unable to cry, unable to yell, bracing myself against the wall.

Was it my fault for wearing this figure-flattering suit?

I do not remember walking the seven blocks to work at the invention company. I don't remember how I made it through my work shift. All I can remember is that when Kai picked me up from work and drove me to my condo in Oakland, I begged him to stay with me that evening. My mood was solemn, and my body trembled as he held me close through the night. Both of us were speechless. Kai didn't ask me any questions, and I didn't volunteer to tell him. He understood that I am the type who will talk about things when I am ready. This time I was never ready.

As the days passed after the incident, I wallowed in pain and embarrassment for not defending myself. Mired in shame, I couldn't muster the courage to tell anyone about what had happened.

I pictured how devastating it would be for take-care-of-home-base Kai. It would stab him in the heart if he knew that this had happened because he couldn't fix the lemon or the croaked Fiero.

I pictured how overprotective Sanjay would worry and hover around me if he knew what had happened.

I pictured my enraged mother dragging me like a ragdoll down to the Port Authority offices where she would demand retribution, like threatening to kick the bus driver's ass. I couldn't bear the idea of this incident becoming a public matter.

So, I sealed my lips in a vow of secrecy, never to tell anyone about this incident. In fact, I never did tell anyone until I decided to write my story in this book to share it with you.

THE WOUND

It was two days after the incident on the bus. I told Kai that never again would I put myself in the position of having to rely on public transportation. As an emphatic declaration, I stated my intention to buy a new car immediately. I was beyond diplomacy at this point. I had to do what I had to do. Next, I called Sanjay to tell him my plans. He connected me to his friend Gary, an auto salesman. Five days later, I financed a car—a reliable, 1989 Honda Accord two-door coupe, five-speed manual transmission, champagne metallic with beige interior. I never rode public transportation in Pittsburgh again.

Another consequence of that traumatic incident was that it started a trend of covering myself up in public. I hid the gentle youthful curves of my slender athletic frame behind baggy clothes and a powerless disposition. My ambition, courage, and confidence were tamed by the shame I felt inside. And in that moment of shock, as I leaned against the concrete wall, I didn't know who I was. I shrank into the shadows of the building towering over me in the downtown street and disappeared. I felt like I'd been reduced to a worthless object. I had no more value to the bus driver than the penny I saw on the ground in front of me. The penny was probably discarded from someone's loose change after some superfluous purchase like a pack of chewing gum or a can of "pop," as we call soda in Pittsburgh.

I was hurt that no one would speak up for me, and I was horrified by the fact that I couldn't speak up for myself. The entire incident reinforced my belief that *I don't matter* and anchored it to a profound feeling of powerlessness and worthlessness from being so degraded.

Nearly three decades later, a man of interest smacked me on my butt during a happy, playful moment. I instantly flared up like a lioness in attack mode and said, "Don't ever do that to me again!"

I had no idea where that came from at the time. The incident on the bus had been repressed in my subconscious memory until this trigger brought it all back to the surface. Thankfully, this man was an understanding and caring person who allowed me the space to be with my emotions. Later, I explained to him that I had been traumatized by an experience in my past and that the smack had reawakened the trauma. He accepted the explanation with compassion and acknowledged my vulnerability. Though, it was far more than a sign of vulnerability; I was being called to heal this wound.

On my journey to heal from this trauma, I learned something powerful about my reaction that day. I had choices. I could choose to accept that the event happened. I could choose to accept that I had choices at the time of the event. I could choose to accept that I had choices after the event. By accepting the role that choice played in this event, I gained tremendous benefits. The biggest of which is that I owned the story and could rewrite it.

In the new version of the story, I am not the damsel in distress; instead, I am the superhero whose inner struggle was won when I embraced my superpower—my Grace. And now, I am armored with a strength I didn't know I had; and the audacious confrontation of my own vulnerable humanity has convinced me that I ready to save the world from the menacing villains of shame and self-doubt. Thus, the reason I have written this book for you.

In *"What Happened to You? Conversation on Trauma, Resilience, and Healing,"* Dr. Bruce Perry, co-authored with Oprah Winfrey, refers to the strength and lessons we gain from our traumatic experiences as "post-traumatic wisdom."[2]

Power Tool 2: *Choose It* has an incredible power to create evolutionary wisdom, among the many other lessons, tools, and good seeds that choosing may grant us.

POWER TOOL 2: CHOOSE IT

We choose the role we play at any given moment in life.

Even in the most traumatic of circumstances, there is a choice in how you perceive and respond to things. One of the most striking examples of this is Viktor Frankl's story of how he survived as a prisoner in the Nazi concentration camps during the Holocaust. Frankl states that even in horrific conditions in which a person is under extreme psychological and physical stress and even when everything is taken from the person, he/she still has a choice.[3] Any person has the freedom to choose his/her own attitude, his/her own way of being, and what can happen to him/her mentally and spiritually.

He suggests that suffering ceases to be suffering the moment we make the conscious choice to bear the suffering with grace. Being dignified, brave, unselfish, forgiving, and empathetic in difficult circumstances—these are choices worth making. And it is when you meet your suffering with this type of grace that you raise the quality of your life to that worth living.

Some say that only by suffering do we know we are truly alive. The Buddha's First Noble Truth states that suffering (*dukkha*) is innate to existence. Our job is to overcome the suffering in life by releasing our painful attachments. So, yes, it's an inevitable part of being human. But you get to *choose* how to play your role in all of it.

There is a collective nature to our humanity. Life is given to us to live as we choose. As individuals, we define our experience by the choices we make. You have a responsibility to choose wisely, regardless of what may be happening around you, not just for your own sake but for the sake of all of humanity. We are all connected, and what we choose to do and say inevitably affects those around us. Sometimes, the best choice is the one that serves the greater good for all.

We have choices even when it appears that we don't.

Sometimes an event is thrust upon you, such as a sudden job loss or a betrayal by a friend or partner. It's not something you would have chosen for yourself; still, you do have a say in how you respond to those unwanted experiences. You also can shape the kind of experiences you will have in your life by making conscious choices. If you think about a recent event that felt somewhat traumatic or challenging, you will probably see that you had choices. How did you find yourself in that situation? How did you choose to respond at the time of the event? How did you choose to feel about yourself or about others after it happened?

Remember that, except in extreme situations beyond our control, there are choices available to you: the choices made before the event, the choices made during the event, and the choices made after the event. You have a choice at any point—even when it appears that you don't. And your only limits are the thoughts you choose to have and the decisions you choose to make. You will rise, conquer, and achieve by choosing to think and act on uplifting thoughts. You will feel miserable and inadequate by choosing to think and live according to disempowering, negative thoughts. In creating your life, you are always making choices. Why not make good choices that serve your best interests?

And, Gorgeous, understand that I am not advocating for you to use positive thinking to override or ignore the traumatic events that occurred in your life—as if to pretend they didn't happen. That approach will only keep you stuck in the past. Take the lessons that these difficult experiences have to offer and understand that you are not made weak because of them. Instead, allow them to set you on your growth path. By doing this work, the negative events of your life will no longer define you and your attitudes.

The journey to wholeness is about arming yourself with your authentic power, owning your truth, and living your empowered life. This is all possible when you align yourself with the idea that the quality of your life is enhanced by the power of choice—reframing your perspective and choosing an empowered view. You have power over the events, circumstances, and conditions of your life. They do not have power over you. Choosing gives you access to this power.

Choice is our saving grace.

While there was no way to undo that traumatic event involving the bus driver as if it had never happened, living in shame and denial had only kept me trapped in the victim role. To end this suffering, I learned to take control over how I chose to perceive MYSELF in that circumstance. First, I acknowledged what had happened to me as well as the pain I had experienced from it. Then, I recognized that it wasn't my fault. I *did* matter. I didn't deserve or invite this kind of mistreatment or disrespect.

As I slowly healed and released all that pain stuffed inside of me, I was able to reframe my experience and see things in a different light. I now understood that I had done the best I could under the circumstances and given what I knew at the time; I had been true to myself. And my actions didn't cause any known harm to another person. As I see it, my actions served the greater good for all involved or who could be impacted. And thankfully, my reaction to a playful smack on my backside by a love interest inspired me to heal my wounds and remove the impact of this event on me.

With this level of awareness, I was able to see the "good seed" in the situation—and most importantly, I saw the good in me. By acknowledging this truth, I replaced powerlessness and worthlessness with a sense of self-worth. Assigning a new meaning to these incidents empowered me to see myself in a positive new light, and it freed me from the prison of shame, self-doubt, and guilt.

When I accepted this truth, I received a gift. I got clear about my superpower—Grace. Grace is like Wonder Woman's bulletproof bracelets. It gives me indestructible power and agility. It serves as my shield and my sword. With grace, I am so powerful that my feminine strength and strong will—my "Toni the Tiger-ness"—balances and supports my inherently loving nature. I can overcome any obstacle and do it in love. So, now that I know the wisdom of Grace, the stories I'd originally told myself that I was powerless and *I don't matter* get to be rewritten.

I am not suggesting that my choices and actions would be right for you. Certainly not. Only you can choose the lessons and good seeds you want to take from your experiences. And when you realize that you have the freedom to choose your response to any given situation, you awaken the power in you. Maybe even a superpower.

Choose wisely. Make deliberate choices aligned with who you want to be, how you want to act, what you want to believe, and what you value in life. You have the power of choice. Recognizing this magnifies your powers exponentially.

> You will never be defeated if you make the choice to take the seed of good from every experience—no matter how traumatic, strange, inconceivable, challenging, or dark.

JOURNEY TO WHOLENESS DESIGN SPACE: CHOOSE IT

DISCOVERY & PRACTICE

Grab your *The 7 Power Tools for Designing Your Life Journal* or notebook and a pen or pencil.

This is your time.

Choose a quiet, sacred place for this meditation where you can be undisturbed and where you feel free, comfortable, safe, and unencumbered by distractions. Find a seated position in which you feel most comfortable, either on a floor cushion or sitting on a sofa or chair. Have lots of drinking water and a box of tissues nearby. Feel free to light fragrance-free candles and dim the lights. Avoid stimulating your senses with visual information, music, incense, alcohol, cigarettes, or any potential distractions. The point is to drop into the space of reflection.

Please note that some traumatic memories may require the support of a therapist or counselor. Trust yourself. If you experience an abnormal level of fear or anxiety on this journey and question "going there" because it may be too traumatic, then consult a therapist and request support in completing this process. It's okay. Your healing is worth it, and so are you.

Take a deep breath, and let's start the *Choose It* process. This process will help you identify the choices you have in the defining moments of your life.

1. What event or situation stands out as a defining moment in your life? (Refer to

the events you referenced in *Own It* and feel free to explore other events as they come up.)

2. How did you respond?

3. How has your vicious cycle played a role in your response?

4. What are other possible ways you could have responded in these circumstances?

5. From today moving forward, what could you choose to do or say instead? How would this new choice empower you?

    * If the new choice does not make you feel empowered, what is holding you back from owning your power?

    * Go deeper. What is the empowered choice you can make?

6. What is the seed of good you can take from this experience?

Rinse (drink water) and repeat. Repeat this exercise for at least two more events that you see as defining moments in your life.

Forgive It!

There are times in life when your carefully crafted persona you use to survive in the world just isn't enough. You think you've got yourself covered until you're suddenly forced to confront a disappointing and humiliating experience or an act of betrayal. For instance, you lose the job promotion to a seemingly inferior candidate. Or you experience a broken trust, like your life partner cheats on you, or you break a promise you made to yourself to never do that thing again!

The pain and humiliation from the experience can be excruciating, like alcohol on an open wound. It gets to the point where you can't stand the pain anymore, so you try to stuff your feelings of shame, blame, and resentment. Unable to process these intense feelings, you direct your pain and anger toward the perpetrator—the boss, the colleague, the lover. You may even begin to direct your negative feelings toward those who resemble the perpetrator; people completely unrelated to the "crime." And you may find yourself flaring up and getting triggered by situations that feel uncannily like the original event.

These toxic feelings can take hold and fester and grow like mold in a wet basement, feeding on itself and multiplying a thousandfold. And it won't stop growing until you let go and learn to forgive. Yes, *forgive*. The most powerful of the "F" words.

You may fear that forgiving someone who harmed you will only make you more vulnerable. You may think it will make you weak. You may think that you will lose your power if you stop punishing the perpetrator. The truth is that you are only hurting yourself.

In this chapter, we explore the Power Tool *Forgive It*, and discover the key to forgiveness. With the Power Tool *Own It*, we developed awareness of our foundational belief and took ownership for our role in assigning "it" meaning. With the Power Tool *Choose It*, we recognized the power of choice and acknowledged that there is a seed of good to be found in every event, however challenging it may be. With the tool of forgiveness, we take a step further in our transformation process.

Forgive It involves taking deliberate action to heal our wounds by releasing negative feelings held toward others and, most importantly, ourselves. Nearly two decades after a superior colleague in our seemingly safe work environment committed an irreverent violation of me and betrayed our trust, I finally forgave him. Only then did I become free.

THE ENDLESS LOVE

I met take-care-of-home base Kai when I was fourteen years old. Over time, our friendship grew into a committed relationship. He was an uber-talented creative type and a trained dancer in classical and modern genres. It was the '80s and modern urban dance then was all about breakdancing. As part of a popular breakdancing group, Kai was one of the best—a pioneer. His quick feet made James Brown look like he was moving in slow motion.

Eccentric and colorfully dressed, Kai was often compared to the legendary musician, singer, and actor Prince. Yes, the Purple One. Among our social circle, it became popular commentary that I was Apollonia (Prince's co-star in the movie *Purple Rain*) to his Prince. I never co-signed this association. I didn't want this type of fame, and I was far from the girl groupie following Kai around with seductive interest. Secure in my role and relationship, I understood why other women—young and old—would lose their minds in Kai's presence.

My relationship with Kai was a beautiful one in so many ways. We shared similar relationship values and built a solid foundation on these values. Still, conflict did arise on several occasions when we realized that our career goals didn't match up. My dream of pursuing a corporate career involved plans for me to leave Pittsburgh. When he wasn't dancing, he dreamed of opening a music studio in the basement of his grandparents' home and perfecting his self-teaching as a musician. On the surface, it appeared that we were different and had different dreams. That was only somewhat true. The conflict rested in Kai's own foundational belief and my *I don't matter* belief. The trigger was too much, causing us to break up twice over the nine years we'd known each other. The second breakup would be final.

I am especially grateful to have had a healthy, loving relationship with such an incredible partner. I wish all women could experience a first-love relationship like the one I had with Kai. I'm convinced that having such an experience would help women know the miraculous power of blossoming in love. Although the relationship ended, my love for Kai will never die.

THE NEW LOVE

Almost one and a half years after Kai and I would finally say "goodbye," I made room for more love. I affectionately call him "Mr. Genius," a fitting moniker since he is brilliant. He's the absentminded professor type; introverted, slightly aloof, humble. A nice guy. Beneath his cool surface, there's a strong fire burning inside of him for equality, diversity, and Black empowerment. I suspect he inherited this passion in his DNA by way of his Black father, who was a leader in the civil rights movement in the 1960s, and his feminist white mother, who stood alongside her husband in the struggle for justice.

Shortly after meeting Mr. Genius in my hometown, he moved from Pittsburgh to Ann Arbor, Michigan, to pursue his specialization in biomedicine. Five months later, I followed him.

Before I could say hello to this new adventure waiting for me, I had to say a lot of hard "goodbyes." I said goodbye to the city that had been my bedrock for understanding life; the only place I had known for twenty-four years. After a four-year career climb from part-time intern to a full-time regional program coordinator at the market research firm, I received a resounding send-off from my supportive group of colleagues. I also received a warm celebration from my colleagues at the radio conglomerate, where I had continued to work on weekends. And I said goodbye to the friends and family who had nurtured me, laughed with me, supported me.

It was hardest saying goodbye to my little sister, who was just twelve years old then. It pierced my heart to see her trademark facial expression of tender toughness get all twisted up as she held back her tears. I promised her that I was only a six-hour drive away and we'd visit frequently. I assured her that I'd always be with her in her heart and sealed the promise with a kiss.

After giving away most of my possessions, I packed what I needed in the folded-down back seats of my Honda Accord, and off I went to Ann Arbor. Six hours later, I arrived in the quaint college town occupied by the University of Michigan (UofM), home of the Wolverines and the maize and blue. There waiting for me was the cool-as-a-cucumber Mr. Genius dressed in knee-length running shorts, his trademark running shoes, and a Nike athletic t-shirt. I already knew how this former track star spent his time while I was driving. Happy for our reunion, we held each other in a long embrace.

Within days, he and I were drawn into the welcoming spirit at the UofM, the pomp and circumstance of college athletics, and the atmosphere of rigorous academics rivaling any Ivy League school. We fit right into the diverse culture, settling easily into our new life together in a cozy little off-campus apartment.

THE GIG

With my heart set on applying to graduate business schools, I had to establish residency for one year in Michigan before I could qualify for in-state tuition. What did I do in the meantime? In typical fashion, I worked three jobs. I worked as a junior-level manager for a national hotel chain and as a babysitter for the cute daughters of a successful couple. And within four months, I landed my third job—what seemed like the gig of a lifetime.

After a successful introduction by a mutual friend and no-nonsense contract negotiation, I earned a short-term freelance consulting gig with a two-partner advertising agency in suburban Detroit. I credit my training in corporate communications at Duquesne University, my background with the market research firm managing the qualitative research development process for forty television and radio stations around the country, and my knowledge of the inner workings of radio for granting me this opportunity. I was brought in as a consultant for strategic business development. The partners were pitching to earn the $8 million budget that two Fortune 500 companies had allocated to target advertising to people of color.

I was on cloud nine. For the first time, I would sit side-by-side with the owners of a company and observe firsthand what it took to run a business. Although I was learning a lot on the job, my communication training, problem-solving skills, and keen insight enabled me to make a significant contribution. I saw and felt the grind, the passion, the pressure. I wear my sensitive nature like a badge of honor, as it enables me to size up moments when compassion and grace are needed. And in my new role, this was a handy skill. I stepped in at the appropriate times, just when the two male partners began bulldozing their way through the challenges of business development. Rather than let their egos lead them down the path to complete macho-hood, I would gracefully redirect their attention to the minority consumer who needed us to show up with responsible advertising that spoke to them. I was proud of my role, and I felt like a valued member of the team.

Going to the office was compelling and fulfilling. Several times a week for almost three months, the three of us sat at a small conference table in a tiny office. We studied trends, built strategies, developed campaigns, and collaborated on proposal writing to woo these Fortune 500 opportunities. My soul was enriched because this little girl from the projects who felt she didn't matter was now at the table making big deals and doing it alongside her own people—Black folks who had upbringings like hers.

Everything was moving along smoothly until I experienced the ultimate act of disrespect. I ended the gig the next day.

THE PARTNER

It was a cold winter Friday night, and the proverbial five o'clock closing bell had rung. One of the partners and I were the only people left in the office. I put on my coat and picked up my purse. As I walked toward the door, I turned to say "goodbye" to the partner at his desk. To my surprise, he was following right behind me.

I was shocked at how close he was. I smiled nervously. Suddenly, he grabbed me, pulled me toward him, and wrapped his arms tightly around my arms, pressing them against my sides. Then, he kissed me. I turned my face and twisted my body in a struggle to release his grip. It was too tight. I kneed him just hard enough to break free, bolted out the door of the storefront office, and sprinted to my car parked outside. I threw the car in reverse; peeled out of the parking space; and shifted through first, second, third, fourth, to fifth gear in a matter of seconds as I raced down the short stretch of road leading to the highway. I violated every traffic rule and tested some of the laws of Physics, making my usual twenty-five-minute commute in record time. Still, it seemed to take forever to find my way home to comfort and safety.

I don't remember grabbing my belongings from the car or locking the car doors that night. I don't remember how I got into the apartment building, whether I used my key or called from the outside intercom. I don't remember entering the door to our apartment. I only remember falling into Mr. Genius's arms as tears flowed down my face like Niagara Falls. My body was cold and shivering. I don't think it had occurred to me to turn on the heat in the car during the drive.

"Toni?" he said with concern.

Tears and shivers were my only response.

"Toni, what happened?"

Still silence. I squeezed him tighter.

I don't know how long he held me like that, but I know it took some time before we made our way to the sofa and a while longer for me to tell him what had happened.

By nature, Mr. Genius was not possessive, protective, or controlling, and he wasn't easily angered or agitated. His temperament had an ease about it, that laid-back manner associated with his Southern Californian archetype. So, he didn't fly into a rage when he heard about what happened with the partner. But I think the news hit him like a dagger in the heart. For many minutes, he did nothing . . . said nothing. Then, his body trembled, and he broke the painful silence with his favorite curse word: "F&%K!"

Traumatized, we both lay awake in bed that night, unable to sleep, unable to speak.

The next day, Saturday, I sent an email to the partner which included a notice of termination of the contract and an invoice for my time. I had copied Mr. Genius on the communication.

On Monday, Mr. Genius escorted me to the agency to gather my belongings and leave a physical copy of the notice of termination and the invoice. To my surprise, Mr. Genius had sent an email to the partner after I'd sent mine. So, when he and I walked through the front door, the partner met us there. The partner vehemently denied his behavior. The mere sight of him— this married man and devoted father—made my stomach ache and tears well up in my eyes. I walked over to the workstation which had served as my desk, and gathered my belongings.

Mr. Genius and the partner exchanged some words which I was unable to decipher. I honestly didn't want to know what was said. I was proud that my man would show up and take care of business. When I approached the front door where they were standing, Mr. Genius held the door open for me and followed me out. We went to the car and drove quietly back to our haven in Ann Arbor.

It took time for both of us to process our feelings and put the pieces of our life back together. We didn't have the emotional intelligence to deal with the situation in a healthy way. We both repressed our feelings, and never spoke of pursuing the matter legally. This was long before the #MeToo movement in 2017, when women were courageous enough to speak up and call attention to the widespread problem of sexual assault and abuse.

About a month after the incident, the partners refused to acknowledge my persistent requests for payment of my invoice. Mr. Genius and I decided that it was not worth legally pursuing payment of the $1,500 invoice in view of the emotional price we'd have to pay in the process of collecting it. So, we stuffed the pain of that, too. And we stuffed the entire experience in the private vaults of our minds never to speak of it again. As I closed the large, heavy door of my vault, the sad song on the soundtrack of my life, *I Don't Matter*, played melodramatically in the background.

Not until my journey to wholeness required that I heal this wound would I finally open the vault and confront this painful memory. Almost two decades after the incident with the partner at the agency, I unstuffed the pain from that traumatic experience. In the process, I also had to deal with the pain from the trauma that had preceded it: the absence of my father, the beatings I suffered as a child, the harassment by Sarah and her posse, the bullying by my classmates, the betrayal of Ricky, the groping by the bus driver. And so, my forgiveness journey began.

Looking back, I could clearly see how these past traumatic events had a direct link to self-loathing, self-criticism, self-doubt, self-sabotage, and even self-neglecting behaviors that I had been experiencing—all of which caused that breakdown in the parking lot at the convenience store on that eerie night before Halloween, decades after most of the traumatic events had occurred.

I could see how my foundational belief that *I don't matter* and the feeling that I didn't belong was causing me tremendous pain. Over the years, this hurt had grown inside of me like mold, until it completely consumed me. I no longer recognized myself and I couldn't bear the sight of myself. I had such a poor self-concept that the belief I didn't matter had become a self-fulfilling prophecy.

Once I saw how I was living my life as if this false reality were true, I realized that I was not meant to carry this burden of emotional pain. I imagined how much easier my life could be, and how much more I could realize, if only I weren't held captive by the burden of shame. I began to explore how to release the pain by inquiring deep within. I gradually let go of the idea that I was a victim, and let go of the blame. What I learned was that I had to bow down—surrender—to the healing power of forgiveness for myself and the perpetrators. And so, I did.

The Power Tool *Forgive It* is about being an advocate for yourself. It involves releasing the negative feelings you hold toward yourself and others and healing your wounds from your emotional pain. This pain steals your precious life by blocking your authentic expression, holding you captive to your suffering. Forgiveness, though, works like a magic elixir, breaking all that free. With *Forgive It*, we learn to let go of the emotional pain to gain something greater—our truth.

POWER TOOL 3: FORGIVE IT

We cannot just forgive and forget.

Before we explore the power of forgiveness, it's important to acknowledge why it's so hard for you to forgive the perpetrator. The proverbial wisdom is, "Just forgive and forget." Let me explain why that doesn't work. To do so, I need to go a lot deeper.

In Chapter 1, *Own It*, we looked at the foundational belief associated with our deepest wounds: *I am not lovable,* or *I don't matter,* or *I am unwanted,* or *I am invisible,* or *I am bad,* or *I am too much,* or *I am powerless,* or *I am a failure (a loser),* or *I am never enough.* Each of these self-limiting beliefs carries emotional baggage along with it, and the root of this emotion is shame. Shame plays many roles in your behavior; and when it comes to forgiveness, shame is the part that keeps you hooked and makes it so hard to forgive.

In her book *I Thought It Was Just Me (But It Isn't): Making the Journey from 'What Will People Think?' to 'I Am Enough,'* Brené Brown, the renowned expert on shame and vulnerability, describes shame as the experience of believing that we are somehow flawed.[4] This makes us feel fundamentally unworthy of acceptance and belonging.

Societies teach people to conform to certain norms and standards. This cultural conditioning is used as a form of control, threatening people with punishment—banishment from society—if they don't conform, if they step out of line, and if they don't obey authority. Shame becomes an inherent part of that belief system.

By nature, humans are communal beings. We feel the pressure to fit in. If in any way we are perceived as different from the norms and standards, then we feel we are punished for being "different"—as outcasts or misfits. When we don't match what's "normal," we feel we don't belong, that we are flawed. To belong and to be loved in a society, a community, is a basic human need in the well-known "hierarchy of needs" established by psychologist Abraham Maslow.[5]

Shame lives in the experience of being flawed and not belonging. Shame can feel excruciatingly painful; and when an experience reinforces the shame attached to your foundational belief, you seek ways of coping. You adopt behaviors to survive in a world where you feel you do not belong. These behaviors become so familiar, even predictable, that they become normal parts of the fabric of your life.

In some cases, the pain from an experience no longer feels like pain because you've become resigned to it, numb even. You may have thought *that's just how it/he/she is*, or *that's just who I am*. Or you may develop coping strategies, such as being cynical, distant, judgmental, angry, passive, or a people pleaser.

In other cases, you are aware of the pain from the experience and feel it acutely daily. To relieve the pain, you may adopt self-destructive behaviors, such as intentionally causing yourself harm (excessive drinking, drug use, eating disorders, promiscuity, self-mutilation, etc.). Or you may express abusive behavior toward others, such as intentionally causing them harm.

Shame is not to be confused with guilt. Both are intense emotions caused by self-judgment in response to an experience, but they are distinct from each other. Shame comes from the belief that "I don't belong" and am not worthy of belonging in the world because "I am flawed." Guilt comes from the belief that either "I have done something" that I shouldn't have done, or "I didn't do something" that I should have done. This distinction is important because guilt can be appeased or alleviated by doing something differently. You can "right the wrong" by your actions, like apologizing or making amends. You cannot just undo shame.

As it relates to self-forgiveness, you may find it is easier to forgive yourself for doing or not doing something (a guilty action or inaction) than it is to forgive yourself for being something you are or you are not (a shameful experience).

> Shame gets attached to your identity and lives with you—in you—as a truth. Really though, shame is not the truth; it is merely residue of an emotional trauma.

When an emotionally charged event occurs, the trauma gets stuck in your body. You can eliminate some of the toxic effects of the shock from your body after the event by crying, screaming, or trembling. But your neuro-system stores the memory in the brain and body to identify a similar threat in the future. Then, anything which feels unsafe or threatening will produce a biochemical reaction akin to the original trauma. The nervous system will kick into high alert and trigger a reaction in the body. This is called the "fight, flight, freeze, or fawn" response.[6] You may confront the threat (fight). You may run (flight). You may become numb and experience an inability to act or move (freeze). You may fold or capitulate (fawn).

In primitive times, humans relied on this instinctive mechanism to survive in the wild. The body had a temporary shift in its biochemistry, readying itself to respond to the threat. After the threat, bodily functions returned to normal.

The human body isn't designed to stay on red alert. Yet in today's world, the psychological stressors we feel in response to our environment keep us in "survival mode," triggering emotional fears, anxiety, stress, and depression. Our foundational beliefs are linked back to an original traumatic event. And when even the slightest trigger reminds us of that event, it engages the emotions entangled in the initial trauma and the pain and shame resurface. It's a subconscious process until you do the work to bring it to your awareness.

As we explore traumatic events in our lives, it is important to acknowledge that the energy you feel about the event is because the event is somehow attached to, or triggering, the initial trauma where you formed your beliefs about yourself. Therefore, it is hard to forgive and forget because the trauma is deeply rooted. While it may be hard to forget, forgiveness is still the goal.

Forgiveness allows us to find a common denominator in our humanity.

The work you've begun with Power Tool 1: *Own It* and Power Tool 2: *Choose It* will help you deescalate the experience of the trauma. You need to get the awareness of the story you've attached to the trauma before you can take the step of forgiveness.

As you've learned so far, your foundational belief is not the truth; your belief and the story you've attached to it have caused you to exhibit unfavorable patterns of thought and behavior. If you can accept that this is true of you, can you accept that others are merely acting out based on their own traumas? Their own shame? Can you see that all of us are just trying to survive in a world where we want to belong? Then isn't it reasonable that you can develop a level of acceptance for yourself and your own stuff? And isn't it also reasonable that you can develop a level of acceptance for other people and their stuff?

Forgiveness is a tool for developing greater acceptance of ourselves and others, and acknowledging that we are all humans living in a world where everyone desires the same thing: to belong. Forgiveness enables us to find the common denominator between people.

Forgiveness causes a momentum shift on our wholeness journey.

Forgiveness involves making a conscious decision to forgive and taking deliberate action to release feelings of resentment and anger toward the perpetrator, be it a person or group.

There may be some concerns that come up for you, such as: If I forgive the perpetrator, won't it make me weak and vulnerable? If I forgive the perpetrator, won't it make him/her try to exercise more power and control over me? The answer to these questions is: No!

To refuse someone forgiveness only shackles you to the hurt and shame you experienced, and it holds you hostage to the perpetrator. When you forgive the perpetrator, you disentangle the emotions of pain, blame, and shame from the event. And you free yourself.

Forgiveness begins a repatterning process because you are now graced with understanding and nurtured by a new perspective. There is a positive impact on your self-esteem, self-confidence, self-worth, and self-reliance. Forgiveness, therefore, creates a momentum of transformation and healing on your wholeness journey.

A Forgiveness Credo provides a set of practices to support us in our journey.

I define below a Forgiveness Credo which provides healthy and supportive guidelines for completing the process of forgiveness:

1. *Let go of the belief that your pain is worse than that of the perpetrator.*

   There is no way of knowing or measuring who holds the most pain, and holding that belief prevents you from releasing your energy toward your goal. The belief will keep you tethered to the idea that you are a victim or that you have been victimized, rather than helping you regain your personal power.

2. *Accept what happened and suspend all judgment.*

   In Chapter 1 *Own It*, we discussed how events by their nature are neutral. The event—the "it"—just happened. Forgiveness asks that you accept that it just happened and remove any judgment as to the rightness or wrongness of your action, the perpetrator's action, or the event itself. Assigning a judgment is one way to give the event a negative emotional charge and fuels the pain and shame that you carry.

3. *Remove any negative emotional charge attached to the experience or event.*

   Give up the desire to punish, demand retribution, or seek justice. Let go of any desire to blame, explain, seek answers, defend, justify, or complain; and let go of the negative emotional charge which comes with these desires. Understand that holding on to emotions is easier than letting go and forgiving. And by staying in the energy of the emotions, you are avoiding going to the place required for your healing. Our goal in forgiveness is to release the pain and shame. This step is crucial for that purpose.

4. *Be ready and willing to forgive.*

You have the power to change how you feel, how you live, what you think, what you do. Anytime. Always. Period. When you harness this power and ready yourself to forgive, you take a gigantic leap forward in your wholeness journey. From this place of readiness, you're sending a "yes" signal to the energetic field around you. This field will rally on your behalf to support your goal. The moment you decide to let go and forgive is the moment you gain access to your biggest reward—freedom from pain and shame.

5. *Accept that we are all human and all of us have flaws and weaknesses.*

You may find yourself seeking "closure"—some subjective and elusive thing that will give you a reason and permission to forgive. This is not really what you need. (I had to learn this lesson the hard way—trust me.) What you really need is "acceptance"—of yourself and others. You serve yourself and others best when you accept that everyone is human and is just trying to survive in this world. Every person—I mean EVERY person—desires to experience love and wants to belong. Everyone makes mistakes and has imperfections; and almost everyone is carrying a painful wound or is limited by certain beliefs and self-sabotaging behaviors. Show empathy for the perpetrator(s) in your life by accepting their humanity and considering that at the time of the event(s) the perpetrator(s) was/were likely disconnected from his/her/their true loving nature. And sometimes—that perpetrator is you. Accept your humanity, too.

6. *Forgive yourself.*

There are many reasons why you may need to forgive yourself. Perhaps you were the perpetrator of an action against another or maybe you have allowed yourself to be victimized by the action against you. Grant yourself grace. Show compassion and empathy for your own humanity. It is easier to forgive others when you forgive yourself.

We are worthy of forgiveness, too.

Why do you sometimes refuse to forgive yourself? Your response may be some form of "I don't deserve it." Well, let's go deeper.

Your foundational belief may be the underpinning of that thought. As stated in Chapter 1, your foundational belief is like a life sentence lived out as a punishment for a crime for which you've already been found guilty. You've already declared yourself to be flawed and not belonging, so why would you change that belief by suddenly forgiving yourself? Another reason why you may not forgive yourself is that you may believe you are "guilty by association." Somehow you may see yourself as responsible for the crime and/or somehow complicit alongside the perpetrator(s). Is it true that you are flawed in the ways your self-limiting beliefs suggest? Nope. Are you already being punished for some action because of your foundational belief? Nope. Are you complicit in the act simply because of your limiting beliefs? Nope. Do you deserve forgiveness? Absolutely.

The foundational belief and all the stories you tell yourself about it simply are not the truth of who you are. The truth is you are worthy of forgiveness, and you are worthy of freedom from the internalized pain involving the event(s) and the perpetrator(s). You are worthy of freedom from regret for what you've done to yourself or allowed others to do to you. You are worthy of freedom from self-loathing, self-criticism, self-doubt, self-sabotaging, and even self-neglecting behaviors. This freedom comes when you heal. And guess what else: you deserve healing. Why? Because you are worthy!

Self-forgiveness provides access to believing in your worth. When practicing self-forgiveness, the most effective tool in The Forgiveness Credo is *Accept that we are all human and all of us have flaws and weaknesses.*

It reminds you that despite your shame triggers—those feelings of not belonging—you are not alone.

> Recognizing our common humanity makes it easy to feel compassion for yourself and others, and it opens the door to self-forgiveness.

When you forgive others, you are granted grace for doing so. And give yourself grace. It's okay. You, too, are human.

A letter of forgiveness is a tool for our healing.

To release the pain from the traumatic events in my life, I started the forgiveness process explained in the "Journey to Wholeness Design Space" at the end of this chapter. For some of my perpetrators, it was easier to go through the process than for others. It was easier to forgive Sarah and her posse than it was to forgive Ricky. It was easier to forgive the bus driver than it was to forgive the partner at the agency. I had internalized deeper feelings of pain when I felt the incident was an act of betrayal by someone who knew me and "should have known better." My pain was deeper because of my negative assumption: Since the perpetrator knew me, then his/her/their behavior toward me only proves what they thought of me. *I don't matter* to them.

To move through the forgiveness stage was a journey, but I was relentless and resolute. The pain of holding onto the feelings was too great; and quite frankly, I was tired of paying the price for the pain. My health and well-being were adversely impacted by the tension and stress I carried while holding on to this pain. I wanted to feel free. I wanted peace. I wanted to live a well-designed life, not the one I had been living, which was by default of my past trauma.

I found that the most helpful step was to write a letter to each perpetrator. The letter was structured to acknowledge that I forgive them, why I chose to forgive them, what forgiveness provides me, and that I genuinely see them as deserving of forgiveness and wholeness. I followed the instructions of the Forgiveness Credo to guide me in what and how to express myself in the letter. Below is the letter that I wrote to the partner at the agency:

Dear [partner],

I forgive you. I forgive you because the love inside of me will not allow me to hold hate toward you. I forgive you because I no longer endorse the story that I am a victim. Holding on to the pain, the blame, and the shame had been blocking me from fully living and fully loving myself. I no longer accept this as my reality. I forgive you because I choose to accept that you are here to teach me a valuable lesson about the power of loving myself and others.

In forgiving you, I am set free. I am free to love, live, and serve. I forgive you because there is a bigger purpose for my life. You are here to remind me of my courage and strength to fulfill this purpose. Because of you, I get to rise up in my power and do what I am meant to do for others. Because of you, I can be a voice for other women who have encountered you or others like you. I get to help these women heal from shame and find their path to wholeness. And I get to be the best version of myself.

I forgive you because what you did doesn't define me. In fact, I accept that your actions are a statement about you, not me. I forgive you because you are human, and you have your own deep pain and fractures from your life's experiences. I wish you great success on your journey as you face and heal from your own transgressions. I wish the same for you as I do for me—unbridled joy, unconditional love, peace, healing, and wholeness.

With love and gratitude,

Tonya

Forgiveness is a practice for the strong.

Forgiveness requires surrender, but it is not an act of weakness or frailty. It's not a show of caving in or giving in.

> Forgiveness is a power move—an act of love and grace that comes from the wisdom of an open heart.

Like a magic elixir, forgiveness releases the emotional pain that weighs you down and steals your precious life. It allows space for your authentic expression, giving you the freedom to live the life you were born to live. This transformation asks that you consciously choose to be forgiving.

Forgiveness is a process. It may take time to forgive some people. There may be some resistance and vacillation because of your shame triggers. That's normal. In time, forgiveness wins over the pain when you *Forgive It*. On the forgiveness journey, you will find your essential truth—the truth that you are not your foundational beliefs, the truth that you are not alone, the truth that you are a beautiful work in progress.

So far in our forgiveness journey, we have worked to disentangle our emotions from the original traumas. In *Own It*, we took responsibility for the meanings we assigned to the events. In *Choose It*, we chose to see the seed of good and assign a new perspective to our role in the events. By taking these steps, we have released ourselves from the emotions of being victimized by the trauma. Now, we can *Forgive It*.

JOURNEY TO WHOLENESS DESIGN SPACE: FORGIVE IT

DISCOVERY & PRACTICE

Grab your *The 7 Power Tools for Designing Your Life Journal* or notebook and a pen or pencil.

This is your time.

Have lots of drinking water and a box of tissues nearby. Avoid stimulating your senses with visual information, music, incense, alcohol, cigarettes, or any potential distractions.

Important note:

A portion of this process involves physical work. Ensure that the environment is not restrictive. You will need freedom to be vocal. You may need space to move your body.

Some traumatic memories may require the support of a therapist or counselor. Trust yourself. If you experience an abnormal level of fear or anxiety on this journey and question "going there" because it may be too traumatic, then consult a therapist and request support in completing this process. It's okay. Your healing is worth it, and so are you.

Take a deep breath, and let's start the *Forgive It* Process.

Before we begin, let's get present to the Forgiveness Credo. This is your guide during this portion of your process:

1. *Let go of the idea that your pain is worse than that of the perpetrator.*

2. *Accept what happened and suspend all judgment.*

3. *Accept that we are all human and all of us have flaws and weaknesses.*

4. *Remove any negative emotional charge attached to the experience or event.*

5. *Be ready and willing to forgive.*

6. *Forgive yourself.*

Identify a highly emotional or traumatic event in your life when you experienced shame/being shamed/feeling ashamed. Give this event a name, for example: *Dad missed my piano recital.*

- Where were you at the time?

- Who was there?

- If applicable, who was not there but was expected to be?

- How did this experience make you feel about yourself?

- How did your foundational belief get attached to this experience?

- Name the shame. How did you feel shame, shamed, or ashamed?

This next set of steps requires you to do physical work. These are the most critical steps in the process. **Participate** fully. It will be worth it. You will speak the responses out loud. You are not writing at this point in the process.

- Who is it that you must forgive? (Create a picture of the perpetrator in your mind.)

- What happened? (Give voice to the events as if you are speaking with the person, in a matter-of-fact way, state the wrongdoing, the violation, the infliction.)

- What actions must you forgive as related to the perpetrator?

- What actions must you forgive as related to yourself?

- What is your pain? (Give voice to the pain and feel the pain. Allow the emotion and let the emotion flow. If you feel a negative emotional charge, then you have not yet reached a place of forgiveness. Let out the emotion—cry, yell, scream, punch a pillow. Release the energy of the charge. Your goal is to move the energy, not dwell in it. Check in with yourself. Do you feel at peace? Do you feel calm? When you do, come back to a sacred mental and physical space where you can re-commit to your willingness to forgive.)

- What kind of pain do you think the other person(s) may have been dealing with at the time of the event?

- What are the most important things you learned about yourself because of this event?

- What are you missing out on because you haven't forgiven the perpetrator(s) or yourself?

- Accept a new belief that you can have everything you are missing. How will you feel knowing you have it? Allow the emotion of this victory to fill you up.

Write a letter to the perpetrator. (Sending it is optional.)

Write down five things you are grateful for because of forgiving the perpetrator.

Rest in love. (Let the love fill the void where the hurt once lived.)

Rinse (cleanse by drinking water) and repeat (with the next person).

You must complete this process again and again until you have forgiven every person involved in each event that you must forgive. And when you complete that, FORGIVE YOURSELF. Forgive yourself for anything that remains entangled in the events you described above. Write a forgiveness letter to yourself. Then, rest in love.

If needed, feel free to catch a breath. You may try some practices for self-maintenance such as taking a walk or soaking in a bath or going for a massage. Give yourself permission to feel both cared for and connected to your inner self.

You are doing great work. This process will reward you.

CHAPTER FOUR

Dream It!

Personal relationships mirror our most vulnerable parts—the parts you would rather hide from than openly acknowledge. When things go wrong in a relationship, you may believe that you have failed the other person in some way or that this person has failed you. Or you may blame some condition for the relationship not working, such as "we're not a good match" or "we grew apart" or "the timing wasn't right for us."

You may feel threatened by the idea of your relationship failing. It's a threat to everything you had built in the relationship, and it threatens your identity—the person who you thought you were in this relationship. Often, you see no way to respond to the threat other than to end the relationship and concede to failure.

News flash: Nothing is "failing." The so-called failure, or stuck place, in your relationship points to an essential insecurity that you are feeling, a sense of lack—not only in your personal relationship but in your life in general. I'm sure that you have experienced this insecurity in a close relationship with a partner, a sibling, a friend; in a relationship with a boss or colleague at work; or perhaps even with a perfect stranger. It becomes most obvious when interacting with a romantic partner. From my experience, it all comes down to that "unanswerable question" we explored in Chapter 1. Your ability to receive an answer would satisfy your essential need for love and reassurance from your partner. However, it's flawed. Your foundational belief will not allow you to receive or accept any answer.

Personal relationships are the most profound "teachers" when it comes to understanding your foundational beliefs. Those beliefs can get in the way of virtually anything you truly want to have in your life. You may dream of having the perfect love relationship, a vibrant healthy body, abundant finances . . . you work hard to make it happen; and yet, it eludes you. You may blame this and that, but really, you're just in your own way. And that's because, at no fault of your own, you're clinging to your foundational belief.

When you become aware of the power of the mirror to show you your patterns of thinking and behaving in a relationship or in the pursuit of a goal and you see how your foundational belief comes into play, your life will change dramatically. You will be free to envision new possibilities and see unlimited potential in your relationships and in your life.

In this chapter, we focus on the Power Tool *Dream It*. You learn about your power to manifest what you truly want with the one thing that you have any control over . . . your thought. Despite the beliefs you hold, you have the power to change your reality. You can create, do, have, and be anything that you want. And it starts with your willingness to dream—even the seemingly impossible dream. It requires a willingness to step out of your comfort zone and to become aware of how your self-sabotaging beliefs are hurting your personal relationships and blocking you from reaching your goals. Until you are free from the behavior, and until you believe it's possible, how can you expect to attract what you truly want? I had to learn this lesson the hard way by going through a divorce.

THE DIVORCE

Mr. Genius became my husband about three years after the incident at the advertising agency. Friendship was by far the strongest force in our relationship. We commiserated over the same things. We shared very similar views on most things; and when we didn't see things alike, we drew upon each other to expand our own perspective. It was richly rewarding for both of us to have this mutual respect, admiration, and consideration in our relationship. Our friendly spirit often left curious strangers thinking that we were siblings rather than love partners when we were out somewhere. But to those who knew us, Mr. Genius and I were a "power couple."

Mr. Genius developed preventative medical practices and cutting-edge biomedical techniques to understand the health issues that disproportionately impact the Black community. He had recruited and trained a diverse group of aspiring cardiologists, exercise physiologists, vascular surgeons, chemists, biologists, and physical therapists. His mission was to promote critical thinking and cultural sensitivity among practitioners in health care. He also deeply desired to inspire a community of high-risk folks to embrace self-efficacy in their overall health care by making lifestyle changes.

We cultivated our relationship built on a philosophy of supporting each other to live our best lives and be our best selves. We nurtured each other's personal and professional dreams and aspirations. In that spirit, I had read many of Mr. Genius's publications. I had also critiqued many of his practice lectures, or "talks" as they're called in his field. Our dinnertime conversations regularly included discussions about ethnic disparities in health care, complex medical topics, human genetics, anatomical functions, diseases, medicines, and alternative treatments.

I learned so much from Mr. Genius that my friends often joked that I was "a doctor by association"—to which I would respond, "I resemble that remark."

Given that I am an advocate of holistic health, it was a label I didn't mind wearing. I liked to be in the company of my husband's genius and to participate in his career passions. It gave me knowledge in areas outside my academic pursuits, having earned a BA in English and Corporate Communications and an MBA in Marketing. I especially enjoyed cheering him on in the pursuit of his dreams, and he was a strong supporter of mine.

Mr. Genius and I loved to laugh; we laughed at the same thing, at the same time, almost every time. Some of the things we laughed about hysterically would only be funny to other closet nerds like us. And some were mainstream, like the bellyaching, fall-on-the-floor laughter we'd experience when watching episodes of *I Love Lucy* or *Martin* or *In Living Color*. Laughter was our medicine, and we took heavy doses of it.

Then, there was jazz. Jazz brought Mr. Genius and me to our happy place. Marriage counselor Dr. Gary Chapman had identified five love languages: acts of service, affirmation, physical touch, quality time, and gifts. And he wrote extensively about these in his bestselling book, *The 5 Love Languages*.[7] Well, I'm convinced that "grooving to contemporary jazz" is the sixth love language that Dr. Chapman overlooked.

We enjoyed the funky soul-jazz of the legendary saxophonist Grover Washington, the progressive rhythms of Gerald Albright's sax and bass, and the sultry keys of Brian Culbertson. I'd hum along to the music while playing air guitar, or sing into a broomstick as my mic, or do a silly jig on the "dance floor," as I called the middle of our living room. Mr. Genius would smile warmly, amused by my shenanigans, bobbing his head to the beat. Occasionally, I'd persuade him to join me on the dance floor for a cha-cha. After which, he'd retreat to one of his favorite corners in the various homes where we lived over the years and start grinding away at his work.

Mr. Genius was an all-around competitive athlete and an overachiever. His greatest competitor was himself. He was driven to beat his last best time and outperform his last best achievement. He had to prove to himself that he could do it, and he was determined to succeed at everything he tried. Anything that threatened to interfere with his goals was cast aside—and that included me. There are issues in Mr. Genius's past that contributed to this behavior. His drive for success was fueled by his foundational belief. This insecurity caused him to create physical and emotional distance between himself and others, and especially me.

By contrast, my foundational belief, *I don't matter*, caused me to clamor for his attention and a deeper connection to him. I felt like I was standing in front of a semi-opaque glass wall he had built to shield himself from emotional connection with others. I could see his shadow behind it, but he could not see or hear me. It makes sense that a woman who convinced herself that she doesn't matter would suffer in a marriage in which she felt unimportant as a wife. Why is that? Because it was a complete self-sabotage. And guess what? It was the same for him—a self-sabotage.

While Mr. Genius was doing the great work that won him many accolades in his career, I was participating in life without my husband by my side. I, too, was having success and winning top accolades and recognition for my interior design work and for my social contributions as a community and industry leader. But I was feeling alone in the process. With few exceptions, when vacationing with my mother and sister, my mother-in-law, or friends, I did most of my traveling alone. I went to black-tie events alone; I showed up to couples' events alone. I did most everything alone. *Alone.* It was like sitting by myself in the cold cafeteria with Sarah and her posse yelling "She ain't all that" all over again.

The more alone and unimportant I felt, the more I tried to distance myself from the pain. I stopped going to places or events that I would have enjoyed because I didn't want to go alone. I stopped spending time with my friends who were couples because it reminded me of my aloneness. This strategy only caused me to feel more alone. Eventually, I lost my usual zest for life and confined myself within the four walls of the home I'd built with Mr. Genius. More than ever, I embodied the belief about myself that *I don't matter*. This belief now seemed justified and confirmed by the day-to-day life of my marriage.

While this was happening in my world, Mr. Genius had become a master at constructing taller and more opaque glass walls in his world. The meaning that I assigned to Mr.

Genius's absence was that *I don't matter to him*. And I questioned my worth. My "I am not good enough" competed with his, as if he were saying, "I am not good enough either."

In retrospect, it's clear that we were focused on finding whatever it was that could make us feel like enough. The problem was that no matter what we tried, it never felt like enough to fill the big void in our lives and our love. In reality, we were more than good enough for ourselves and each other. The stories we made up about ourselves kept us thinking that something was wrong . . . that we had to fix it . . . that we had to prove something to each other.

We were looking for acknowledgement from each another, but shame got in the way. For years, we struggled to get the answer to our burning, pervasive,and unanswerable questions of each other, the essence of which was: *Do I belong and fit in with you in the way that I need to feel that I belong and fit?*

In this psychological interplay between our desire to love and our desire to be right about our beliefs, we rejected any answer to the question. We just kept validating our foundational beliefs, which left us feeling powerless. We knew there was something more for us as a couple, but we didn't know how to go about finding it. Quite frankly, it felt risky. Confronting whatchamacallit would be like letting go of a piece of ourselves; some part that we thought was protecting us, something that we thought defined us. Keeping that safe was easier than peeling away the mask to explore our truth.

Despite going to counseling and trying other types of support for couples, we didn't have language to understand the shame, sabotage, and unanswerable question. We didn't have the insight to know how to resolve our hidden fears. Nor did any of our therapists, counselors, or coaches. So, what could we do? We came to the only "logical" conclusion: we were in an unworkable situation.

And we resigned ourselves—as many people often do—to accepting the loss of a great love. That was that. After five years together prior to marriage and nearly sixteen years together in a marriage, and despite our friendship that lasted even through all the painful times, Mr. Genius and I concluded that divorce was the only answer to our dilemma.

If Mr. Genius and I had understood our shame, our self-sabotage, and the dynamics of our unanswerable questions, our relationship might have become everything we had dreamed of when we first married—a strong relationship built on a philosophy of supporting each other to live our best lives and be our best selves.

What I learned from this experience was painful and it cost me dearly. I did, however, find the seed of good in it. It showed me the way back to my truth and opened the path to discovering the wholeness journey I share with you in this book.

To have what you truly desire—whether in a romantic relationship or in your career, your health, your family, your finances—you must become aware of how you're standing in the way, as it is your foundational belief that is likely playing out as a form of self-sabotage. Doing this work is a surefire way to become a match for your dreams.

With Power Tool 4: *Dream It*, you learn more about your self-sabotaging behaviors. And you will explore how the toxic trio of control, shame, and self-doubt arising from your foundational beliefs is the dream killer. By becoming aware of the thoughts and patterns that don't serve you, you develop the ability to direct your thoughts and energy toward the realization of your dreams. When you do this, not only can you change your relationships, but you can also create a new destiny.

POWER TOOL 4: DREAM IT

Our unanswerable questions exist to validate our identity.

Most breakdowns in personal relationships are rooted in a sense of shame arising from the foundational belief you hold about yourself. The belief also shows up in everyday circumstances as trivial as when someone cuts you off in traffic. You may get triggered and think the driver is a self-serving jerk and your justification is rooted in your foundational belief.

He cut me off. He must think he's more important than I am. That I am less than him. Notice the reason: *He must think he's more important than I am. That I am less than him.* That's indicative of a person who holds a belief *I don't matter.*

Another could be: *He must think he's better than me.* That's indicative of a person who holds the belief *I am never enough.*

You most likely have a common complaint rooted in your foundational belief. In your reaction to the driver, you are living out a story triggered by your fears and justifying it with the complaint. Likewise, the aggressive driver is living out some core pattern of behavior he developed to protect himself psychologically from his own fears.

In intimate circumstances such as a love relationship, when you express disappointment with your partner, whether verbally or non-verbally, you are likely living out some version of your core belief about yourself. The reason for your disappointment is not really the issue. This disappointment is rooted in your foundational belief and the need for your partner's acknowledgement and validation. One of these questions identified in Chapter 2 *Choose It* lies at the heart of this issue:

Do you love me?

Do I matter to you?

Do you want me? (Or will you leave me?)

Do you see me? Do you hear me?

Am I a bad person?

Am I too much for you?

Am I powerful (strong) enough for you?

Am I successful enough for you? (Am I a winner to you?)

Am I enough for you?

You may occasionally ask your partner the question. Mostly, though, you do not ask the question. Instead, you will look for the answer to the question reflected in your partner's words and actions. For example, let's assume your partner doesn't take out the trash.

If you are seeking the answer to the question *Do you love me?*, then you may conclude that he doesn't love you because he did not take out the trash.

If you are seeking an answer to the question, *Do I matter to you?*, then you may assume that you aren't important to him and that is why he doesn't take out the trash.

If you are asking the question, *Do you see me?*, you may assume that he is not taking out the trash because you are invisible to him.

You get the idea, right? The complaint that you have about why he isn't taking out the trash is a clear indication of your belief about yourself. (If you were unable to identify your foundational belief and related unanswerable question in the "Journey to Wholeness Design Space" in Chapter 1 *Own It!* and Chapter 2 *Choose It!*, perhaps this chapter has given you more insights. You may want to go back to those earlier chapters and take a deep dive.)

What if he said to you "I love you" every day and your foundational belief is *I am unlovable.* Would you believe him? If you are being honest with yourself, the answer is "No." You do not believe him because your foundational belief has convinced you otherwise. It's understandable and no fault of your own.

When the people or situations around you provide affirmative feedback to the questions arising from your foundational belief, you reject the answer. Your belief system will not allow you to accept the answer because this answer threatens the validity of the belief. See, the belief system has become synonymous with your identity, and it would cease to exist if it were proven wrong. How could you live without it? Who would you be then? But wait . . . it's even more than that. The belief convinces you that YOU would die if you do not hold the belief any longer. It's a tricky little thing.

So, now what? You want to survive. And in these moments, you cannot comprehend anything else, so you reject the answer. You make the question unanswerable not because there is no affirming answer to the question, but because you reject the affirming answer. It is not a riddle; it is a real phenomena in your brain, happening more frequently than you may be willing to see or acknowledge.

We must look beyond the reasons we give to find the root cause of a "failure."

The idea of living without your foundational belief is way too vulnerable a thing to even comprehend. Even though it feels vulnerable to expose the belief, it is more painful and seemingly life threatening to live without it.

Understanding this, look back at a failed relationship. You may have named a reason to justify the loss of that relationship. Still, dig deeper. You may find that your relationship ended because you could not get a satisfactory answer to the questions behind your beliefs. Because you didn't get the validation you needed (to feel loved, important, wanted, seen, heard, good, powerful, like a winner, enough), your frustration built to the point of disconnection from your partner; and in time, the inevitable happened. You said, "We fell out of love." Or "We grew apart." Or "He was selfish." Or "He was never around to help raise the children." What really happened was you lived out a self-fulfilled prophecy of the secret you wished most to hide—your foundational belief. It goes something like this:

"I knew I was unlovable; that's why he does not love me."

"I knew I didn't matter; that's why he ignored me."

"I knew I was unwanted; that's why he left me."

"I knew I was bad; that's why he would rather be alone than with me."

"I knew I was too much; that's why he would hang out with the guys rather than with me."

"I knew I was invisible; that's why he didn't see me (or hear) me."

"I knew I was powerless; that's why he took advantage of my kindness."

"I knew I was a failure; that is why I failed at this relationship."

"I knew I was never enough; that's why he was never happy with me."

This dynamic not only plays out in your romantic relationships, but also at work, or when you commit to a new goal (a New Year's resolution perhaps), or face a new challenge. The reasons you give for things not working have more to do with your identity than it does the reasons you give.

The first requirement to fulfill our dreams is to step out of our comfort zone.

The foundational belief has been your comfort zone. To change your experiences, you'd have to be willing to step outside of your comfort zone, but you're afraid. It's scary—even daunting—to imagine how to let go of your self-limiting beliefs and to accept the answers to those unanswerable questions because that's become your identity . . . your comfort zone.

It's a paradoxical situation. The comfort zone where you hide in the shadows to protect yourself from others and conceal your wound is the very place where your suffering is rooted. The wound results from your shame—the feeling of being flawed, disconnected, insignificant, left out, or different. When you open the wound, it stirs up your insecurities. The pain of it all causes you to run, pretend, cover up, shield, isolate, and become invisible. You then feel alone again, swallowed up in shame once more.

On the inside, you are nestled under the covers and hiding. On the outside, you are living in a world of make-believe, pretending to be something you are not, wearing your masks to ensure that the wound inside is not exposed. You convince yourself that by staying in the comfort zone, you're in control. Let me tell you otherwise; the comfort zone is the place of your suffering.

When we let go of the need to control, we gain it.

It doesn't take much for us to get forced out of this comfort zone and feel out of control. This experience of feeling out of control is the key condition for suffering.

What does it mean to feel out of control? Let's consider some examples of control as it relates to an intimate relationship. When you don't get your way with your partner, it feels like you are not in control. Or when your partner does not meet your expectations or give you what you want, you may feel out of control.

It isn't simply the loss of control that causes this suffering. The story you tell yourself about the experience in which you feel out of control leads to suffering. You get attached to the pain of the experience and use it to affirm your insecurities. You then express the pain by exhibiting behaviors such as complaining, judging, crying, blaming, ridiculing, arguing, etc. Herein lies the hook: the attachment to the pain and suffering creates the conditions for being a "victim."

Your need for control causes you to suffer. When you let go of control, you gain ease and perspective about your circumstances . . . your life. If you can learn to recognize the moments when you want control and can release your attachment to it, you will be free to gain what you desire. By releasing control, you invite that which is for you to show up.

The Universal Law of Conservation of Energy states that energy is neither created nor destroyed; it can only be transferred. This means that energy in a system will remain at the same level of intensity until it is transferred to another form. If you want to have different results, then you must change the energy within the system requiring the new result. Rather than trying to control the thing, let it go. Release it. It will find a new form aligned with your new level of energy—your desire—and show up in alignment with you. This applies to your desire for a healthy relationship, vibrant health, abundant finances, a thriving career . . . any desire.

You can transform your suffering by (1) understanding the role your foundational belief plays, (2) releasing the emotional pain of the wound and stepping out of your comfort zone, and (3) letting go of control. When you take these steps, you are less likely to transmit this wound of pain and suffering to your family, your community, your loved ones, and even a stranger.

But how can you push through the suffering and step out of your comfort zone to realize what you really want?

The answer: *You dream.*

When we dare to dream, we change our lives.

It may sound like a bold leap, but it's been proven that when you allow yourself to dream and you act on those dreams, you can dramatically improve your life.

When you close your eyes and are in a dream state, these dreams can help you to identify and resolve issues that get buried in your unconscious mind. The "dreamwork" (as psychotherapist Sigmund Freud called it) creates pictures of what needs to be healed in the psyche, and this can be an effective tool for self-healing.

For our purposes though, the Power Tool *Dream It* is about conscious dreaming, or intentional visualization. You use the fluid space of the imagination to create something you dream of having in your life. The act of conscious visualization stimulates the part of the brain where patterns, impulses, and motivations are stored. Because the subconscious mind cannot distinguish between the real and the imagined, you can shape your reality and repattern your brain by using your imagination.

Think of something that you truly desire or wish to have but haven't yet realized. Maybe you desire a strong partnership, or you want a new trajectory in your career, or you want to lose thirty pounds, or maybe you desire to increase your income by twenty percent. Why haven't you achieved the goal? What's holding you back?

Your automatic answer may be "fear." This is a common response. And it is only partly true. Let's take it a step further. Your foundational belief is likely what's getting in the way of realizing the dream. See, your fears are a condition of your default thinking. And what is the source of your default negative thoughts? Your foundational beliefs. Your foundational belief can hold you like a prisoner in the comfort zone, restricting your self-expression, your ability to love, and your ability to dream. And it blinds you to the truth of the magnificence of who you are and what you can have and achieve.

Here are some clues that the foundational belief is at work and blocking you from having what you want: You may feel resigned and think things will never change. You may feel indifferent, like you really don't care that much about this or that. You may lack enthusiasm, experience uncertainty, be indecisive, worry, procrastinate, and avoid things. You may have issues with self-control or be overly cautious. Those are fear-based responses. Look more deeply. You will find what is really blocking you from realizing your dreams: the inherent characteristics of your foundational belief, which are insecurity, shame, and self-doubt. These are dream killers. But what is the antidote? Passionately using your imagination to bring what you want into reality.

If you apply your imagination to create a vision for yourself and then act on it, you can have the thing that you desire. You do this by controlling your thoughts. Even though your thoughts seem to run wild, you can control them. You have the inherent ability to think whatever you want to think. You have the power to direct your thoughts to create anything that you can imagine.

> You can direct your mind toward thoughts that kill the dream, or you can direct positive energy toward visualizing the dream. You have a choice. Why not choose to dream?

Our dreams are held in the desires of our hearts.

If you applied your imagination and could be anything you want to be, who would that be? I venture to say that you would choose something other than the foundational belief you currently hold about yourself. Yes?

Inside of you, there is a desire for something more. It's okay to desire more. The abundant universe has the resources to satisfy every desire. Desiring is allowed and encouraged. The mere fact that you have a desire for something is evidence that the thing is for you to have, to experience, to be.

> Dreaming empowers you to access your heart by discovering the things you love and most desire.

When you shine the light on your dream—and believe with all your heart that you can create whatever you want to have, do, and be—a magical thing happens: you set in motion the potential to achieve your dream.

Dreaming is a tool for us to live without limits.

When you create a strong positive vision and hold the image in your mind, your subconscious begins to confirm it as your reality. You can train the subconscious to energetically support your vision by keeping it strongly in the forefront of your thoughts. Universal laws will be on your side, too; wherever the focus of your thought goes, energy flows. You will find the world conspires to give this dream to you. Just as your previous experiences were consistent with your limited thought patterns (the vicious cycle discussed in Chapter 1), the universe will conspire to manifest your big, bold, beautiful vision. It's about the energetic force in nature to draw like to like. The universe responds to what you give your attention to and what you hold in mind as an expectation.

The Power Tool *Dream It* involves using your powerful imagination to cultivate a vision of what you would love to have, do, and be. Then you set your mind on this vision, using it as a goalpost to manifest what you want in your life. This doesn't mean that your conditioned thinking and old beliefs will totally disappear. It means that you can change your thoughts to align with a bigger possibility that you see in the areas of your life you want to change or improve. With this bigger vision, you evolve in your journey toward wholeness as someone who understands that the power of thoughts can actualize dreams. This is an unstoppable power and is unquestionably effective for living a life of your own design.

Let's review the work we've done so far in your journey to wholeness:

- Power Tool 1: *Own It* helped you to become aware of the primary negative thought pattern—the foundational belief—that dominates your experiences of yourself relative to the world around you.

- Power Tool 2: *Choose It* gave you the basis for understanding the defining moments in your life and enabled you to see the choices you made in response to those events.

- Power Tool 3: *Forgive It* encouraged you to make forgiveness a priority and supported you in developing compassion for yourself and others.

Accomplishing the work of these three power tools has a cumulative benefit. This work removes the blocks to your self-expression, your self-fulfillment, your self-respect . . . blocks that were the basis for your insecurity, shame, and self-doubt. Removing these blocks frees you to say "Yes!" to yourself, your true expression, your desires.

Now that you are no longer saying no to yourself and being stopped by your foundational belief, you can create an empowered, fulfilling life of your wildest dreams. Really! You have full permission to design your life using your big, bold, bodacious imagination! There are no limits to the imagination; there are no limits to your dreams. So, *Dream It!*

JOURNEY TO WHOLENESS DESIGN SPACE: DREAM IT

DISCOVERY & PRACTICE

Grab your *The 7 Power Tools for Designing Your Life Journal* or notebook and a pen or pencil.

This is your time.

Choose a quiet, sacred place for this reflection where you can be undisturbed and where you feel free, comfortable, safe, and unencumbered by distractions. Find a seated position in which you feel most comfortable, either on a floor cushion or sitting on a sofa or chair. Have lots of drinking water and a box of tissues nearby. Feel free to light fragrance-free candles. Avoid stimulating your senses with visual information, music, incense, alcohol, cigarettes, or any potential distractions. The point is to activate your imagination.

Take a deep breath. **Smile.** And let's start the three-step *Dream It* Process.

Step 1: Clear any blocks

You have stated reasons to yourself and maybe to others as to why you have not achieved certain dreams and goals.

1. What are those reasons?

2. How do these reasons relate back to your foundational belief?

3. How are these reasons acting as blocks to your dreams?

4. What are you attempting to control?

5. What is the big lie that you believe about your comfort zone?

6. By letting go of control and stepping out of your comfort zone to get what you really want, what becomes available to you?

Step 2: Dream Big

You have been given a beautiful gift called imagination. It is from your imagination that you can identify your dreams. You can tap into the pictures in your mind of the things which most excite you, the things which most delight you, the things which most inspire you, the things you love the most. You define the vision by the pictures in your mind when you ask yourself "What do I love most?" and you marry them to emotions you feel which are expansive—like happiness, joy, gratitude, love. When crafting a big, bold, bodacious dream, you are led by love not logic. So, what do you love?

Imagine that it is <u>three years</u> from now and your life is completely different than it is today. What does your life look like?

Allow the pictures to appear in your mind.

1. Think about your <u>health and fitness</u>, what do you desire most? Allow the picture to get vividly clear. What do you see? What are the emotions you feel when you see yourself in this picture? Write it down.

2. Think about your <u>romantic relationship</u>, what do you desire most? Allow the

picture to get vividly clear. What do you see? What are the emotions you feel when you see yourself in this picture? Write it down.

3. Think about your <u>career</u>, what do you desire most? Allow the picture to get vividly clear. What do you see? What are the emotions you feel when you see yourself in this picture? Write it down.

4. Think about your <u>financial life</u>, what do you desire most? Allow the picture to get vividly clear. What do you see? What are the emotions you feel when you see yourself in this picture? Write it down.

5. Think about your <u>family and home life</u>, what do you desire most? Allow the picture to get vividly clear. What do you see? What are the emotions you feel when you see yourself in this picture? Write it down.

6. Think about your <u>social life</u>, what do you desire most? Allow the picture to get vividly clear. What do you see? What are the emotions you feel when you see yourself in this picture? Write it down.

7. Think about your <u>leisure time</u>, what do you desire most? Allow the picture to get vividly clear. What do you see? What are the emotions you feel when you see yourself in this picture? Write it down.

Now that you have created a mental image of your dreams and written it down, you are to put it in a form that you can connect with it every day. Be that by creating a vision board, or committing what you wrote to memory, or recording yourself reading what you've written in an audio app. Your goal is to connect with your vision every day.

Step 3: Expect to Fulfill It

In Step 2, your inner voice has spoken. These dreams came from within you. This means that they are your dreams and no one else's. This dream is normal and natural. This dream is a form, a representation, of your personal evolution. Now, you must expect it to be realized. Believe in your dream. Pause and show gratitude for your dream and the abundance universe that rallies with you in support of having it. Now, watch what happens as we move through the next chapters of this book.

Rinse and repeat. Repeat the assignment until you have created a comprehensive dream vision for the seven categories in your life.

CHAPTER FIVE

Become It!

Every living thing in the natural world, no matter how small the organism, has a life force that drives it towards its true purpose—that which it is meant to be. Inside the lotus seed buried in the muddy waters of a pond is the life force that makes it bloom into a beautiful lotus flower. The same is true of the acorn, whose life force directs it to become the mighty oak tree. Pierre Teilhard de Chardin, French Jesuit priest, philosopher, and scientist, used Aristotle's term for life force—"entelechy"—as being ". . . inside all of us, just as a butterfly is in the caterpillar."[8]

There is a dynamic force in everyone calling us to become all that we are meant to be. Unlike the lotus seed, acorn, and caterpillar, human beings have a consciousness that allows us to tap into our individual creative power. And as such, we are called to manifest—better yet, to become—whatever our spirit, our soul, inspires us to realize in life. This is our life purpose. It is always there, always beckoning us to fulfill it, though many of us (maybe even you?) are unaware of this call and may even refuse to heed it.

In life, many things occur to block you from fulfilling your purpose. You will inevitably have adversities and circumstances—the job loss, the loss of a loved one, the divorce or breakup, the financial setback, the health event—and you may allow these things to overshadow your purpose. The adversities may seem so overwhelming that you lose sight of your "why." Your foundational belief may step in at these weaker moments to deter you from pursuing your calling, or perhaps the circumstances block you from knowing it.

In this chapter, you are reminded that adversities in life are what help you build your strength as you press on toward your purpose. Just as the caterpillar must undergo a seemingly brutal metamorphosis to become a butterfly, you must endure and overcome certain things to fulfill your purpose. Oftentimes, what you think makes you weak is precisely what will make you strong, resilient, and ready for the next challenge. Your life is not weakened by your struggles, trials, or confrontations. Instead, you build new strengths as you overcome them. Conquering the challenges to your growth is a necessary part of the process of becoming; it gives meaning and purpose to life.

With the Power Tool *Become It*, you will listen for the calls that beckon you to become more, and you will find your purpose . . . your true destiny.

My greatest lesson in "becoming" came when I finally confronted my nemesis—the poverty mindset! This enabled me to see how my self-limiting beliefs were getting in the way of my success, self-worth, and self-concept.

THE HAVE-NOTS

As a child, I made two observations that shaped my beliefs about money. First, I observed my mother laboring hard to earn money and make ends meet. I drew the conclusion that making money was hard work. Secondly, I overheard conversations about two types of people: the "haves" and the "have-nots." And I concluded that because we lived in the projects, we were the "have-nots." The haves lived somewhere different. I had no context for "the haves" and couldn't internalize what that meant until I had my first experience in the suburbs when I was eleven years old.

Mama and I were invited to the home of Bill and Betty, a white couple from our church, for Christmas Eve dinner with their extended family. To my eleven-year-old self, the half-hour drive to their suburban home felt like we were driving across the country. The driveway to their home looked like it was a city block long. Entering the foyer of their center hall colonial home was like I'd walked into a mansion. This upper-middle-class lifestyle was something I'd only seen on television before that moment.

The kids were dressed in their Christmas finest, with wool sweaters and well-pressed khakis or skirts. The men wore Brooks Brothers button-down shirts and slacks. The women were decked out in colorful knee-length dresses cinched at the waist. The large dining room table had been extended to fit all of fourteen of us; it was decorated with a holiday-themed tablecloth, floral centerpieces, and fine China at each place setting. The tree in the adjacent living room glistened like no Christmas tree I'd ever seen before. It was thoughtfully decorated with layers of delicate porcelain ornaments and the occasional painted clay or paper snowflake ornament handmade by a child.

I observed every movement and detail within eyeshot, and every bit of chatter within earshot, as the adults collaborated in placing crystal bowls and platters heaped with ham, turkey, stuffing, potatoes, cranberry sauce, and peas, all at the center of the table. We all sat down together. There was a moment of silence before giving grace, so quiet you could hear a pin drop. Betty said a prayer, and then each family member shared a gratitude moment. Many of the kids, all of whom were younger than me, said they were grateful for their presents or their pets. I was grateful that my mom had allowed me to share Christmas with them. Then, in synchronized motion, the women began passing plates and serving the food.

Everything about this experience felt different from what I knew . . . the formality of the gathering, the way they passed the plates, their upright postures as they ate their food. My mom and I looked different. The life we lived in the projects was different. I had now witnessed firsthand the disparity between the haves and the have-nots.

While it is true that going to Bill and Betty's home had clarified the systemic issue of race and wealth for me, this experience also exerted a positive influence in that it motivated me. I saw the world as so much bigger than my little concrete jungle. I became curious about what else was out there for me to see, experience, and learn. This caused me to demand more from myself in order to fit into the world I had been a part of that day.

I became aggressive about my education, challenging my mom to allow me to exercise more influence over my educational path. I learned that night that Bill was a lawyer, and I decided that I wanted to become a lawyer like him. So at age fourteen, I enrolled in a high school that had a Law and Public Service program. Then, at sixteen years old, Mama enrolled me in Urban Youth Action, an after-school vocational training program where I received workplace training which prepared me for a job in the legal field. The program found a position for me with a two-partner law firm. As a "court runner," I would deliver important legal documents to the clerk of courts and ensure that documents were properly certified, stamped, and filed.

By my senior year, I had decided that lawyering wasn't for me, based on my experience of taking case classes in high school and making observations at the law firm. However, the experience itself was life-changing. I had declared a goal and fulfilled it. It set a little fire under my feet, and I began to consider my other dream—to be one of only two members of three generations in my family to earn a college degree.

It's ironic how it was at an institution of higher learning that I would get my second lesson about the disparity between the haves and the have-nots on day one.

THE LOADING ZONE

It was the first day of my freshman year at Duquesne University and I was moving into the dormitory. I pulled up to the dormitory loading zone, driving my mother's burgundy 1988 Oldsmobile Cutlass. In tow were Mama, my six-year-old sister Boo, and enough of my personal belongings to almost fill the trunk of the car. Directly in front of me, there was another freshman in the loading zone, surrounded by her family who were happily and lovingly helping to unpack the trunk of her family's luxury SUV. With about four times the amount of stuff that I had, the newbie was exuberantly negotiating the unloading of her stuff. To the right of me was a similar picture—mom, dad, grandparents, and even more stuff. Behind me, the same.

School hadn't even started and already I felt out of place. This was no place for me, a girl from the projects. I, the "have-not," did not have a lot of stuff, nor an entourage, nor any pomp and circumstance to welcome me to this life-changing event. Graduating in the top five percent of nearly two hundred students in my high school class and being named to the National Honor Society were of no consequence now, as I was a "have-not"—attending an expensive liberal arts school was a daily reminder of this fact.

Unlike most of the other students, I had to work multiple jobs to pay my tuition, buy books, and feed myself. To mitigate this feeling of not fitting in, I moved to an apartment off campus the next semester.

Etched in my memory of that first day in the new chapter of my life is the feeling of shame. It was marked by the hopelessness, isolation, and inadequacy I felt as being a "have-not" in a world of haves. This underlying belief shaped my money story; the perfectly constructed, self-built glass ceiling of my story of lack assured me that I would never have enough to be one of the haves.

THE BANKER

Seven years later, after earning my MBA from Michigan State University, I worked as a consultant for an office furniture company. It was there that I fell in love with interior design. Inspired to pursue my interest in design, I made a course correction and left the corporate life for a regional sales management position to get closer to the customers. I headed to Maryland, where Mr. Genius, who had moved there three years prior, had already set up a nest.

Within fifteen months, I validated my passion for interior design and set myself on a mission to build a decorating business. To explore this entrepreneurial venture, I mustered the courage to walk into a bank and ask to speak with a specialist about business financing options. After a short wait, I was greeted by a man, a six-foot-tall-Brooks-Brother-suit-wearing-forty-something of European descent. We shook hands and introduced ourselves by first and last name. I will refer to him as Mr. Banker.

Mr. Banker invited me into his office, decorated with textured royal blue wallpaper; a cherrywood workstation complete with a desk and return, and a matching hutch; multi-colored speckled carpeting; and fluorescent lighting in an acoustical grid ceiling—not unlike most banking environments in the early 2000s. He gestured with an open hand in the direction of one of the wood-framed chairs upholstered in fabric with a red, green, and blue acanthus leaf pattern.

There I sat, opposite Mr. Banker, tall and poised on the edge of the chair. This was a cue to tell my *I don't matter* and "have-not" mindset that it was time to handle business. I searched to find my words. When I opened my mouth to speak, nothing came out but my breath freshened by the mint I had enjoyed during my wait. I pressed out a nervous half-smile.

Breathe, Tonya. Just breathe.

"I am interested in learning more about financing options for my business," I said, relieved to have spoken the rehearsed sentence.

"Tell me about your business. What type of business is it?" Mr. Banker responded.

"I am planning to open an interior decorating business."

"So, you are not conducting business currently?"

"I have not officially opened the business. Until a few months ago, I was working in corporate America. I found my passion for interior design a few years ago after pursuing my MBA and while working as a management consultant for the world's largest office furniture company in Michigan."

This was an attempt to demonstrate my business acumen and credentials. Mr. Banker seemed unimpressed.

He asked again, "So, you are not currently operating the business?"

"I am not. I am considering purchasing a franchise. It allows me to buy into a proven system. It also provides a support network that can position me for greater success than if I went out on my own to launch a design firm. I am interested in a loan to finance the purchase of the franchise."

"Well, Ms. Comer, we do not have loan products that match your needs. We do not have products for new startups. The products that we offer are for business owners who have been in business for at least two years."

Huh? I didn't see anything like this while conducting research on financing the business. This couldn't be so.

"So, you have no programs for startup businesses?" I questioned in disbelief.

"We do not."

Breathe, Tonya. Breathe.

"Well, how then does someone like me secure funding through your bank?"

"We do not offer loans for new businesses. Our business loans are made available through the Small Business Administration, and they do not have loan products for startups."

After a bit more redundant dialogue, I felt my body getting weighed down from the seemingly unsupportive, unsuccessful, and unsatisfactory results of this conversation.

Breathe, Tonya. Breathe.

After passing a business card across the desk in my direction, Mr. Banker stood up at his chair as if to deliver the final blow.

"Ms. Comer, please visit us in two years after you start your business. We can talk then about your needs for capital."

I stood up, firmly shook Mr. Banker's hand, and followed with, "Thank you for the information and for your time. Have a great day."

"Good luck with your business, Ms. Comer. Keep us in mind for the future."

I tucked the business card into my purse and walked myself out the door.

Mr. Banker had said that he had "no products to offer me." I took that to mean, "No. I have nothing to offer you Ms. Inexperienced-Uninformed-Girl-From-The-Projects-Who-Doesn't-Matter Comer."

He had said to "keep us in mind for the future," but what I heard was, "In fact, lady, don't you ever come back here and ask me a silly question like that again. Loan YOU money? Hum. You are not worthy."

I walked out to my car in a show of confidence but felt utterly defeated as I drove away. Although the bank branch was just minutes from my home, I never returned to that branch again. In fact, I was so discouraged by this letdown that I didn't go to another bank to request capital. I quit. I gave up. I was afraid. It would be too unbearably painful to have to confront my insecurity again.

THE SELF-IMPOSED GLASS CEILING

It was February 2002, and I had just recently been laid off from my job at the office furniture company. The fallout from the September 11 attacks had significantly impacted the U.S. economy and layoffs were commonplace. The seed of good: I got a severance package. I used it to finance the purchase of the franchise and establish my interior decorating business. After five years, I would relocate with Mr. Genius to Philadelphia, cancel my contract with the franchise owner, and open an interior design business under my own name.

Over the years since 2002, whenever business issues came up that could have been resolved by reaching out to a bank for a line of credit or a loan to support my growth, I refused to do it. I hadn't built a safety net financially, so when hard times came, which they did several times in my many years in business, I was paralyzed. Because of my long-term insecurities about my self-worth (still holding onto the beliefs that *I don't matter* and I am a "have-not"), I refused to go to a bank—or to anyone for that matter—to ask for financial help. I was not willing to risk hearing "no" again. *Absolutely not. Nope. I won't do it!*

The cost of these decisions and behaviors was that I suffered in the business. I was always stressed. I was unable to talk about my finances with anyone, not even my accountant, without fear of judgment. This left me feeling alone and without a sounding board to help me solve my problems. I was making poor financial decisions that were costing my company six-figure losses annually. Eventually, I was deep in credit card debt from using them to stay afloat during the down periods.

So, when I found myself on the phone with Katie begging her to accept me into her program to save my business, I was facing losing everything. Lots of things needed fixing—especially my self-worth. The negative patterns of thinking I'd developed were the culprits behind my suffering and despair over the state of my finances.

From the outside, my business appeared to be a success. It looked like I had it all together. The truth is that I was undercharging for my services and overextending myself to keep my clients happy while losing money in the process. I had little discipline when it came to billing clients. I billed a client for only forty hours when I had offered two hundred hours of my time. This was a common practice for me. It was complete self-sabotage, though at the time I was unaware of what motivated that behavior. To keep the story that I am a "have-not" alive, I had to relive the patterns of my "less-than" belief system again and again.

Even though I had achieved enough success to drive a luxury SUV, had the means to fill my trunk with lots of stuff, and occasionally had an entourage and some fanfare, I still felt the shame, hopelessness, isolation, and inadequacy I had felt that day in the loading zone at Duquesne University. While time had passed and I had long since removed myself from that experience, I had allowed it to define me.

THE REFRAME

The time came when I was ready to tackle the self-limiting beliefs that I had developed as a girl growing up in poverty . . . the one who thought she did not matter. I had to face whatever it would take for a "have-not" to become a match for having the life of her dreams and being the woman she was born to be. This meant that I had to be willing to let go of the beliefs that *I don't matter* (my foundational belief) and that I am a "have-not" (my circumstantial belief.) I had to stop allowing my past experiences around my worth and value to define me.

My self-concept was that I was a "have-not" who didn't matter. The truth is that I am in fact valuable, and I matter very much. This fact spoke so loudly to me one day when my greater purpose was revealed: to share my story with you. And by writing this book, I could help women find their way from shame and self-doubt to love and wholeness. I saw clearly that united together, we could launch a Global Love Revolution. I realized that only a person who *matters* can have such an assignment.

Saying "yes" to my purpose was like allowing the caterpillar in my cocoon to break through and become a butterfly. I got to have colorful wings and the freedom to fly.

All those dark moments in my life, from feeling "less than" to being bullied and feeling like a "have-not," shaped my journey of becoming. All of it paved the way for me to be completely in awe of my purpose when I found it. I couldn't imagine any other truth than the one before me.

Throughout my life, I saw plenty of evidence to confirm my significance and contribution. But I was unable to accept it because of my belief system—that vicious cycle—that kept me tethered to a false reality of who I am. Today, I am extremely grateful for my journey. I wouldn't change one thing. Everything has been a steppingstone, paving the way for me to become the woman who has a message and a mission to serve women . . . to serve you as you read this book.

In the journey of becoming, when we discover who we are, we can easily answer the million-dollar question: *Why am I here?* Your path has led you to this place and time for you to become all that you are meant to be. Most likely you will learn, as in my case, that your foundational belief serves as a guidepost to help you find your purpose. The belief you have held as your truth your whole life, the very thing that has defined you and stood in your way, is just a lie waiting for you to call its bluff.

We will explore how to move beyond your false beliefs about yourself, to discover your purpose, and to live your truth in the Power Tool *Become It*.

POWER TOOL 5: BECOME IT

We all have a story of becoming.

You can be everything you are meant to be—all that you are called to be. The power and genius inside of you desires to be expressed fully. Finding that which is inside of you is simply a matter of knowing where to look.

Even before you embarked on this journey of finding your wholeness, you were in a story of becoming that which you are meant to be. In your evolution, you cannot escape your past experiences, nor should you want to. The work of transformation is not about transcending your identity, your stories, and your beliefs; that would defeat the purpose.

> You can't just put a spit-shine on your shame and buff out the painful experiences that marked you. This pain must be acknowledged for you to get the strength you need to grow beyond it.

It's when you acknowledge your pain and observe it for what it really is that you are released from its grip, freeing you to find the truth of your being . . . the truth of who you are to become. Knowing these truths is when you find wholeness.

The truth shall set us free.

This wholeness journey is all about becoming who you truly are. It's vulnerable work, which involves discovering, accepting, and surrendering to that which is calling you. To identify and heed this calling, we must acknowledge the truth.

Often what you define as your truth isn't really true; it's just a story, contrived based on what you and others make up about who you are. While this story is an essential part of being human, it has consequences when we accept it as "our truth." These consequences are that we live a default, surface-level life as reactionary beings in a world of stimuli.

It's easy to misinterpret your persona (the face you show the world) as the truth of who you are, and think of your shadow self (the shame and repressed emotions you want to hide) as your true expression—your authentic voice.

Your persona is carefully crafted by you and made up of your personality, behaviors, and "strong suits." You know what I mean by that, right? These are the unique strengths and talents you developed to be liked and to succeed in life. The persona is a construct we invent as we receive feedback from the world around us.

On the other hand, your shadow (the part of yourself most difficult to accept) holds your pain. It holds the emotional residue of traumatic events you have yet to fully process. As we have established in Chapter 3, this emotional residue is shame. And to cope in the world, we develop patterns of behavior associated with these emotions. These fear-based behaviors are what show up in our daily actions, thoughts, beliefs; they also show up as our "fight, flight, freeze, or fawn" reactions when our traumatic memories are triggered. When your shadow gets triggered, that's telling you your shame wants to be heard and understood. Unless you are willing to explore these dark emotions when they come up, they get projected outwardly in unhealthy ways or they fester within you. At some point, and in various ways, these bottled emotions erupt and affect every aspect of your life.

In Chapter 3, I told the story of how my shadow reared its head during a playful moment with a love interest, triggering the memory of the traumatic incident involving the bus driver. My shadow intruded explosively. By contrast, when it came to being a financially thoughtful business owner, my narrative of *I don't matter* and I am a "have-not" caused me to withdraw and burrow into my hiding place, resulting in decades of unhealthy beliefs and practices regarding money. This cost me financially, but the greatest cost was the loss of my self-worth—my true value. I was blind to my essential truth.

No matter how much success I gained in the material world, I couldn't relate to myself as anything other than a "have-not." It had become so much a part of me that I even resented and rejected the notion I could be anything more. And, as we've explored quite a bit already, self-sabotage will ensure we keep our belief systems alive. So, there I was a successful business owner who was broke, in more ways than one.

Neither your persona nor your shadow convey your truth. Both are fabricated for your survival. Your truth lies in your soul, the essence of who you are. Your truth is something you will not need to sculpt, craft, run from, or hide. Your truth is just that: the truth.

To see your truth, you must be willing to acknowledge both the characteristics of your persona *and* the inner workings of your shadow. The truth of your soul is held in the space between these two parts. Finding this truth is essential to wholeness. As your ever-present soul evolves during your inner search for your truth, you become whole. You will appreciate the lessons of the old stories when you recognize the role they play in helping you to become who you are meant to be.

And then there is the day when we get the answer to "Why?"

Through the journey of ups and downs, victories and losses, good and not-so-good days, all roads can lead you to your life purpose if you are willing to heed the call and explore the "why" for your life.

When your why is revealed, you will undoubtedly see the significance of the steps in your life journey that got you to that point. You may even have an a-ha moment and feel uncontrollable bliss. And guess what?

> When you find your purpose, your first thought will not be a denial, "Oh, but I am invisible . . . not lovable . . . not worthy of it . . . " Your first thought will likely be empowered, inspired, and positive. It will be followed by a big fat, "Yes!"

You may be thinking, well, that all sounds great, but how do I go about finding my life purpose? Let's explore what this looks like from a big picture perspective. The best way to find your purpose is to get clear about the things that really matter to you and why they matter to you. Then, ask yourself who you would have to *become* to solve that problem or make that contribution. Here are some examples of clear purpose statements:

I am put on this Earth to be a voice for the voiceless.

I am put on this Earth to be an advocate for the poor.

I am on a mission to ensure that no child goes hungry.

I support women who have been in abusive relationships.

I help abandoned children find families to love them.

I help women entrepreneurs build seven-figure businesses.

I help minority vendors get equal access to capital.

I bring beauty to the world through my art.

I bring happiness to the world through my music.

These examples are designed to inspire you. To know your purpose and make a clear statement like this, you may have to look deeply into your mind, heart, and gut. The purpose of this chapter is to help you to find out what you are born to do. When you do, you will be like the caterpillar who transforms into a beautiful butterfly.

Let's look at the steps of our journey to wholeness so far: You've owned your role in the stories you've created about your life (Power Tool 1: *Own It*). You've taken responsibility and acknowledged that you have a choice in all matters (Power Tool 2: *Choose It*). You've taken steps to forgive yourself and others (Power Tool 3: *Forgive It*). You've created a vision for limitless living (Power Tool 4: *Dream It*).

And now, with Power Tool 5: *Become It*, you are tasked to acknowledge your truth, identify your purpose, and define who you would have to become to realize it.

JOURNEY TO WHOLENESS DESIGN SPACE: BECOME IT

DISCOVERY & PRACTICE

Grab your *The 7 Power Tools for Designing Your Life Journal* or notebook, and a pen or pencil.

This is your time.

Choose a quiet, sacred place for this meditation where you can be undisturbed and where you feel free, comfortable, safe, and unencumbered by distractions. Find a seated position in which you feel most comfortable, either on a floor cushion or sitting on a sofa or chair. Have lots of drinking water and a box of tissues nearby. Feel free to light fragrance-free candles and dim the lights. Avoid stimulating your senses with visual information, music, incense, alcohol, cigarettes, or any potential distractions. The point is to drop into the space of reflection.

Take a deep breath, and let's start the *Become It* Process.

This process involves three steps, each requiring meditation.

Step 1: Find your truth

Set an intention for this practice: "My goal for this meditation is to find my truth."

Begin by setting a timer for just <u>fifteen minutes</u>.

1. Take three deep breaths, inhaling and exhaling at an intentional but effortless pace. Say to yourself: Until now, I have known myself to be _____. *(Fill in the blank which a list of attributes to include both your persona [strong suits and strengths] and your shadow side [behaviors of your shame triggers.])*

2. Be present and listen to what comes up. Allow the thoughts and emotions—the fear, the sadness, the anger, the regret, all emotions. Do not judge them. Do not dissociate from them. Do not avoid them. Do not assign meaning to them. Simply observe them. If you catch yourself in a mental dialogue reflecting on the content of your thoughts, pause and focus on your breath. Allow your breath to be the cleanser. Take three deep cleansing breaths to reset your meditation. Then gently direct your attention back to whatever comes up.

3. After you see clearly the stories you've lived with as your truth, let's get to the heart of it. Let's define the real truth. Ask these questions: Who am I really? What is my truth?

4. At the end of the fifteen minutes, write in your journal about what you discovered. What did the voices of the identity and the shadow-self say to you? What feelings came up for you? What is your truth?

If you need more time, you will complete this mediation again for another fifteen minutes after you complete Steps 2 and 3.

Please trust the process. Follow these steps as proposed. It will serve, and you will serve yourself.

Step 2: Define your Why

Set an intention for this practice: "My goal for this meditation is to connect with my purpose."

Begin by setting a timer for just <u>fifteen minutes</u>.

1. Take three deep breaths, inhaling and exhaling at an intentional but effortless pace. Ask yourself these questions: Why am I here? How am I to serve? What am I to give? Where in my life have I done something that has made a difference for someone or something and that lit me up.... made me feel alive? What lights me up?

2. Be present and listen to what comes up. Allow the thoughts and emotions. Do not judge them. Do not dissociate from them. Do not assign meaning to them. Do not avoid them. Simply observe them. If you catch yourself in a mental dialogue, just pause and focus on your breath. Allow your breath to be the cleanser. Take three deep cleansing breaths to reset your meditation. Then gently direct your attention back to whatever comes up.

3. At the end of the fifteen minutes, write about what you discovered in your journal. What did you hear or see? What feelings came up for you? What is your purpose?

If you need more time, you will complete this mediation again for another fifteen minutes after you complete Steps 3 and then 1. Follow this order exactly as recommended.

Step 3: Determine your next evolution in becoming

Set an intention for this practice: "My goal for this meditation is to determine my next evolution in becoming in order to fulfill my purpose."

Begin by setting a timer for just <u>fifteen minutes</u>.

1. Take three deep breaths, inhaling and exhaling at an intentional but effortless pace. Ask yourself this question: Who do I have to become to be a match for my purpose?

2. Be present and listen to what comes up. Allow the thoughts and emotions. Do not judge, avoid, or dissociate from them. Do not assign meaning to them. Simply observe them. If you catch yourself in a mental dialogue, simply pause and focus on your breath. Allow your breath to be the cleanser. Take three deep cleansing breaths to reset your meditation. Then gently direct your attention back to whatever comes up.

3. After the timer chimes marking the fifteen minute time lapse, write about what you discovered in your journal. What did you hear or see? What feelings came up for you? What is your next evolution in becoming? What is required of you to be a match for your purpose?

If you need more time, you will complete this mediation again for another fifteen minutes after you complete Steps 1 and 2. Follow this order exactly as recommended.

Rinse (drink water) and repeat. Repeat the mediations in sequence until you have the answers required for each step: What is your truth? What is your purpose? What is your next evolution in becoming?

CHAPTER SIX

Love It!

Our society places great value on appearances. This is especially true for women. From the moment a girl enters this world, she is judged by her physical appearance. Then she may grow up focused on her self-image—trying to measure up to some ideal of perfection—at the risk of losing her true self. The face she presents to the outside world may get confused as her identity. She may even disregard her true feelings and desires to the point of pretending to be something she is not. Underneath, she wants to belong... she wants to feel worthy of love and admiration.

The messages a woman gets every day tell her that she must be beautiful; she must have a perfect figure; she must have gorgeous hair, exquisite eyes, plump lips, and a button nose. Even those who model this standard of beauty, who look stunningly beautiful on the outside, often suffer on the inside from a sense of lack and insecurity (haunted by their own foundational belief). Whether this physical beauty comes naturally or via the handywork of a cosmetic surgeon to achieve the ideal perfection, she still may never feel whole. She focuses on her outer self at the expense of her inner self, which is crying out for authentic expression, for love and acceptance in a world where beauty is idealized and romanticized. She is looking for validation on the outside, when the place to look is deep within, to her inner truth.

With Power Tool 6: *Love It*, you will learn to embrace all of life and fall in love with yourself— just as you are, your parts seen and unseen. You will know that in the difficult times in life, your broken dreams and your seemingly broken parts are there to help you learn how to love yourself more deeply and become all that you are here to be. Your imperfections, missteps, and so-called failures teach you to love yourself—who you really are—and they guide you to awareness of what is most important in your life and is your highest purpose: *To Love.*

The *Love It* power tool raises the bar in your journey to wholeness. It's a significant growth move to accept and welcome everything in your life as a blessing. So far, you've accepted that you made up a story about yourself (*Own It*). You've learned to make better choices by reframing and choosing what you want to experience (*Choose It*). You've also learned to see that all people are flawed and to forgive them and yourself, for the flaws are part of being human (*Forgive It*). These tools help you to overcome the sense of victimhood, shame, and blame. Next, you learned to focus on manifesting what you want in your life through the power of dreaming (*Dream It*). And you learned to heed the part of your soul which is beckoning you to live your purpose (*Become It*).

To *Love It* involves learning to love yourself and everything in your life. This will allow your journey to take you all the way to your highest self-realization. Your goal is to recognize that everything in life is here to teach you lessons that help you to evolve into your highest self. This shift in perspective makes it easy to know, feel, give, and accept love—for yourself and for others.

When I was seven years old, I was asked (as most kids are at that age), "What do you want to be when you are older?"

In my soft little girl voice and with stars in my eyes, I replied, "I want to spread love around the world."

I didn't know what that meant back then. But judging by the example of my heroes Dr. Martin Luther King and Nelson Mandela, I knew it meant something big. Throughout my life, I sought out love in the most peculiar places and found it. I offered love in the most genuine ways and was also rewarded for it. But it took me to go on this wholeness journey to find what the little girl inside of me desired most. With *Love It*, I found my way back to love—starting first with loving all my imperfections—and then was empowered to love others in a whole new way.

THE HEART OF THE MATTER

In the months following my separation from Mr. Genius, I feared the inevitable loss of my friend, my confidant, and my marriage. I was doing my best to move forward with my life and to stay just one step ahead of my next big emotional breakdown. I tried to create new routines and power my way through tough times as usual. But the stress and heartache would prove to be too much. I had not yet reached the point of understanding how dark times can open the way to a powerful new awareness. Eventually, I would come to see this seeming "failure" as a blessing—showing me who I am at the deepest level.

One morning, as on most mornings, I went down to the fitness center in the basement of my building to check off the first task on the to-do list:

☐   30-minute workout

After my workout, I began to race up the stairs from the fitness center to my fourth-floor loft. I suddenly lost my breath. I felt like I was suffocating, and a sharp pain gripped my chest. I stopped on the third-floor landing and grabbed the railing post with my left hand. Within seconds, I felt my body go limp and my cell phone slipped from my right hand, crashing onto the concrete landing. Gasping for air, I felt my body collapse and fall slow-motion to the floor. Then everything went black.

I don't know how long I was unconscious. Not long, I think. When I opened my eyes, I was startled and scared. Shivering and moist with sweat, my slender body was twisted like a pretzel on the cold concrete. My head was only inches away from the lower step. When I noticed my breath, I was grateful. Grateful to breathe. Grateful to live.

Grasping the post of the staircase, I slowly and carefully grabbed my phone, which was close by my head, and pulled myself up from the floor. When I stood up, I felt normal, with no obvious pain. I checked myself out. All my parts seemed to be in the right place. I checked my phone. It seemed to have survived the fall, too. I raised my right leg and placed it on a step. Nothing felt out of the ordinary. Slowly and gingerly, I began climbing the flight of stairs. My breathing was slightly restricted, but otherwise, I felt like myself. I managed to walk, cautiously, nearly seventy feet up to my loft. Once inside, I made my way over to the sofa, laid down and closed my eyes while saying a prayer of gratitude.

About thirty minutes later, I called Mr. Genius. He asked the necessary questions that a medical professional would ask. I assured him that I was well enough to get myself to the hospital; and he concluded that it was safe for me to drive the three miles to the emergency room. He left work immediately and met me there. A two-night stay in the hospital for testing and evaluation was followed by a six-month-long journey of further medical tests for my heart and lungs and a false diagnosis of Pulmonary Sarcoidosis. All of which caused quite a stir for me and Mr. Genius.

In the end, I never received a medical explanation from the doctors as to what had happened to me that day. Thanks to Mr. Genius's professional clout, I received care from some of the best health practitioners in Philadelphia. The only logical explanation we had for the heart event was that it was brought on by a heightened state of stress. As we explored in Chapter 3, the human body is not designed to live in a constant state of high alert of "fight, flight, freeze, or fawn" with its extreme biochemical changes in an active state. The constant presence of the stress hormones pumping through our system alone during this hypervigilant survival mode is enough to cause illness, disease, and even death. So, the explanation is a reasonable one—given my frame of mind.

This event occurred on the anniversary of the fifth month of my separation from Mr. Genius, and four months before I would seek help from my lifeline Katie after my breakdown in the convenience store parking lot. The pain of the events leading up to the separation—the anxiety, fear, resistance, denial, resentment, self-doubt, sleepless nights, and agonizing shame—it was all too overwhelming.

My anxiety during that time of my life was all-pervasive. As is common for people in situations like mine, there were a host of irrational fears. I was anxious about how I'd manage my life without my partner in nerdy chatter, bellyaching laughter, and jazz. I was concerned about how I'd navigate the world without him. And most especially, I wondered how I would look to the world as a divorced woman. I was concerned about checking the box on some random form that would assign me a new label: "Divorced." Or worse, "Single."

I could cover up my insecurity with a mask, but I could not hide the fact that I was no longer co-creating a life with Mr. Genius. I could hide it for a period. In fact, he and I both did. But I couldn't hide it forever. I was afraid that my divorce would mark me with yet another scar among those that already rendered me imperfect (in my view). These concerns about my new identity compounded my stress almost to the point of a nervous breakdown.

THE PERFECTLY IMPERFECT

I felt so flawed by the events of the past that had wounded my self-esteem and triggered my shame. And my more recent confrontations with *I don't matter* had weakened me: the imminent fall of my marriage, the financial distress in my business, the fear of never being able to have the life of my dreams.

I believed that the scars I carried on the inside were also visible on the outside. It got to the point where I couldn't bear to look at myself in the mirror. I was afraid that I was so flawed, so "ugly" from the scars, that a grotesque alien figure like something in a sci-fi movie would be staring back at me. I learned how to apply my foundation, eyeliner, and mascara without using a mirror. If I had to look in the mirror, I would look right through it without even seeing myself. It was completely involuntary; I didn't even know I was doing it. If you have never experienced anything like this before, it would seem inconceivable. But it is a real phenomenon, and it happens to many people with real or imagined physical scars. They can become invisible to themselves.

I had also become quiet, timid, nervous, aloof—characteristics that were inauthentic for me. I had become someone I didn't recognize. No wonder I didn't want to look in the mirror. My self-image was marred, and my sense of who I was had been turned upside-down. I didn't know how to confront the outside world when I felt so conflicted about my identity. The world seemed like a foreign land, and I was a stranger in it.

Later, I would realize that my hyper-perfectionism and concern for how I looked to outsiders was a rallying cry for help. More than anything, I wanted to be accepted and to feel that I belonged. I had an overwhelming need to feel like I mattered when the circumstances of my life seemed to suggest otherwise. *How could I find a place of belonging when I didn't even feel I belonged to myself and I didn't recognize the woman I had become?*

Along my healing journey, I would learn that this drive for perfection blocked my spiritual growth. It got in the way of realizing the true perfection of my inner self. Attempting to be "perfect" is an inauthentic form of expression. My shadow self was provoking this need for perfection. It tried to shield me from being hurt, from being found out. Perfection-seeking was merely a means of trying to hide my insecurity; it was a mask.

While in my healing process, I was proud of myself when I took down the walls that separated me from my inner self, from my purpose, and from others. I felt comforted by the realization that I could give myself the love and nurturing I was seeking from others. I felt most connected to myself when I could see the wisdom in my imperfections. Once I understood this wisdom, I reconnected to my inner self.

On my journey, the *Love It* tool helped me to learn to love myself—regardless of and because of my imperfections. I also learned to love others in a new way—regardless of and because of their imperfections. I also learned to love the world in a whole new way—regardless of and because of its imperfections. I learned to love imperfection . . . to just *Love It!* All of it!

THE LOVE CONNECTION

Despite my years of pain and hurt, loss and aloneness, I've had an abundance of love in my life—incredibly enriching, knock-your-socks-off love with romantic partners, and rich loving connections with family, friends, and even strangers. I have had a deep love affair with the miracles of the world— seeing people survive horrific events, like a person escaping a wrecked car on the side of the road just before it went up in flames; or hearing courageous stories of people defying the odds, like Erik Weihenmayer, the first blind person to climb Mount Everest; or reading stories of dolphins saving the lives of surfers. At such times, I feel an oozing-out-of-my-pores love from the joy of being alive.

In my deepest, darkest moments of despair, it was love that kept me alive. Left to my own devices, I may have ended my own life during those trying times. But moments of love's pure bliss would always, in some miraculous way, shine its light on me. It would make me smile for a few moments . . . just long enough for love to fill my heart with compassion and remind me that even though I may feel that *I don't matter* there is a purpose for life. And that purpose is to love.

The love inside of me desired to expand beyond my inner circle, community, and professional network to reach more and more people with this message of love. I was awakened to the fact that I am here to use my gifts and my triumph over the past to spread love around the world. I call this mission my Global Love Revolution.

This book is my invitation to you to join me on this mission of love. The Power Tool *Love It* will guide you on steps to take to accept and love yourself fully. It will then empower you to accept and love others, too. When you do this, you will not be able to contain your desire for love.

> Love is an infectious, contagious energy. You cannot help but want to share it with others and they cannot help but want to share it with you.

So, let's get to *Love It*.

POWER TOOL 6: LOVE IT

Self-love strengthens us.

You are on a journey to wholeness. Fundamental to being whole is loving yourself. The most important person you should desire to love is yourself. One of the most important teachings of Jesus is, "Love thy neighbor as thyself." This teaching is often misinterpreted. It means that you can only love others to the same degree you love yourself. Equally true is that your neighbor can only love you to the degree you love yourself. So, the key to love is to start with loving yourself.

Before we can go further in this concept of self-love, let's break down the three most used concepts in this world of the identity of "self."

Self-image is the mental picture you hold of yourself—how you see yourself and how you think others see you. It is reflected in what you see when you look in the mirror. The result is a picture of your physical appearance, personality, behaviors, capabilities, skills, values, and principles. If you hold a positive self-image, you focus on your assets, strengths, and potential. If you hold a negative self-image, you focus on your flaws, faults, and limitations.

Self-esteem is how you feel about the mental picture you hold of yourself. In other words, it is how you feel about the self you see in the mirror. Self-esteem is rooted in the emotions you hold about yourself, especially emotions about self-worth: being good enough, deserving, or worthy, as we defined in Chapter 1 *Own It*. Self-esteem is a measure of how confident we feel based on our emotions and our own assessment of our worthiness and intrinsic value. We hold strong emotions related to our self-worth and these emotions influence the things we choose to pursue and our satisfaction with the results of those pursuits. A person with low self-esteem may likely hold low self-worth. A person with high self-esteem most likely holds high self-worth.

Self-concept is a more comprehensive evaluation of the picture you hold of yourself; it is how you perceive your personality traits, values, and behavior in comparison to a standard or "ideal." It relies heavily on the outside world for judging, comparing, and measuring yourself. It influences your moods and attitudes, what you think about yourself, and who you believe you are as a person based on the feedback you receive from the outside world.

Your self-concept is strongly correlated with your foundational belief, which is the homebase for shame and self-doubt. As we discussed in Chapter 3 *Forgive It*, shame arises from our belief that we do not fit in to the outside world. And because you are seeking to feel better about yourself, to fit in, to feel connected, you then look outside of yourself for validation, approval, permission, and love from others. Self-doubt also relies on an external view. If you hesitate to take action—to go for that job promotion, or start that business, or register for that educational program, or speak publicly in front of an audience, it is not your ability or skill or talent that you doubt. You are more concerned about what others will think, do, and say than about what YOU will think, do, and say. Self-doubt is rooted in your self-concept more than it is in your abilities.

How do you improve your self-concept? You change the picture you see of yourself in the mirror. And how do you change the picture?

First: *Accept your imperfections.*

> Our imperfections shine a light on the truth.

Our weaknesses, flaws, failures—the things we want to hide from in shame—are essential to who we are. The point is not to try to separate from these imperfections, or overcome them, or ignore them, but to acknowledge all of them. It is the nature of being human that we have imperfections.

By doing inner work, you can embrace your imperfections. This inner work is not always pretty—it is often messy, uncomfortable, confronting, confusing, and emotional. Yup. And in the process, your life can seem that it's been turned upside down, inside out, and scattered about. It can be disconcerting. Yes, it can, but it is so worth it!

> When you do the work to accept your imperfections, your love expands—it wraps itself around you in a long embrace and teaches you to love yourself and others in the most profound way.

Accepting your imperfections allows you to have more love in your life. You will see and feel love in the little things, the big things, all things. It is such a beautiful thing. You don't want to miss it.

When we see an imperfection, it is in our best interests to *Love It!* And understand and embrace it as our humanness. Let it teach us how to be more of who we are . . . and how to love more deeply. Our imperfections are what make us likable, relatable, trustworthy, compassionate, understanding, and loving. Our imperfections make us who we are.

Second: *Embrace all of yourself*

See yourself fully for who you truly are. You are not your self-limiting beliefs (insecurities, shame, self-doubt.) Embrace all of yourself, all of who you are. Accept yourself as you are with your strengths and your limitations, your highs and your lows. Know that you are perfectly designed to fulfill your purpose, and that your seemingly imperfect parts are necessary for you to do your life's work. And then, build affirming beliefs as the basis for your new self-concept.

Third: *Forgive Yourself*

We explored this in Chapter 4 with the Power Tool *Forgive It.* Still, it deserves to be repeated here. When you accept yourself as you are, you must forgive yourself. With forgiveness, you find compassion. In that space of compassion, love and self-love are present. When you love yourself, you no longer need to seek validation, approval, permission, and love from others. Self-love strengthens you. It transforms your life, allowing you to realize your highest potential so that you can contribute what you're called to do during your time here on this Earth.

Our highest purpose in life is to love.

Experiencing personal triumphs in the wholeness journey leads to an audacious opening of your heart. Your life's journey is meant to awaken you to the love inside of you. Every pain, every joy, every high, every low, every win, every loss—everything serves you. Every moment in your life presents an opportunity for you to learn the ultimate truth: You *are* love. Love is the essence of being human. And from a spiritual perspective, love is all there is.

When you choose love, you choose the good life.

Love is not just a feeling, or something to fall into or out of, or something to get from another, or some reciprocal emotion earned because of a deed. Love is a way of being. It is a practice and a choice; and love is transformational. Love works accepts things and people just as they are; and simply because of the all-powerful energy of love, it makes everything better for all involved. When you choose to act in love, you are transforming life for all things around you… simply by being love. And this includes improving life for yourself.

Learn to love and accept yourself fully. By awakening to your self-love, you develop true compassion for yourself and others; you heal the wounds that separate you from others and tear down the walls that block your love for them. You know what I mean about the walls, right? Those walls created by your shadow self, which are made of fear, shame, guilt, self-limiting beliefs, grief, blame, anger, and contempt.

This may sound lofty and maybe even a little woo-woo, but a necessary part of spiritual growth is to find self-love and then open yourself wide to experience the sacred process of uniting with others in love. Your work is to illuminate and awaken your highest self, the "God" in you that is love.

Unconditional Love is the ever-present force of God within us.

Unconditional Love is the God (Spirit, Infinite, Universe, or whatever you call it) that abides within everyone. To know and experience this divine source of love is our birthright. Yet many of you may not feel worthy of it. Your relationship with a holy practice may come with shame and guilt baggage, leaving you feeling bad or inferior. Perhaps for you, the notion of having to repent for your sins has left you feeling guilty and powerless. Or maybe you were taught to be subservient, which made you feel worthless. Or maybe the idea of being fated by bad karma has made you feel hopeless. No matter what you've experienced, these are lies about you and your worth.

The truth is that as a spiritual being you are whole, perfect, and complete. And in your physical realm, you are to live a good life, fulfill your purpose, and do good deeds in service to the greater good. There is no easier way to do good deeds than by recognizing yourself as a spiritual being who is perfectly made and full of Unconditional Love. This unconditional source of love is within you, always there, moving through you, unchanging, eternally abundant.

Our journey to wholeness begins and ends with love.

Your path begins by waking up to your past trauma and discovering its impact; and it proceeds by resolving into forgiveness, committing to a new dream, and becoming your truth. Your individual path will inevitably lead to a collective love; the spirit of Unconditional Love inside of all of us. By embracing this concept of Unconditional Love and the evolution of your life, you also accept the evolution of the lives of others. This is an important concept because to love is to accept and to accept is to love.

Love is a way of being and it is an action. Choose love. When you choose to be love and give love, you spread the most supreme emotion. The energy of love has the power to heal this world and its pain.

JOURNEY TO WHOLENESS DESIGN SPACE: LOVE IT

DISCOVERY AND PRACTICE

Grab your *The 7 Power Tools for Designing Your Life Journal* or notebook and a pen or pencil.

This is your time.

Choose a quiet, sacred place for this reflection where you can be undisturbed and where you feel free, comfortable, safe, and unencumbered by distractions. Find a seated position in which you feel most comfortable, either on a floor cushion or sitting on a sofa or chair. Have lots of drinking water and a box of tissues nearby. Feel free to light fragrance-free candles. Avoid stimulating your senses with visual information, music, incense, alcohol, cigarettes, or any potential distractions. The point is to drop into the space of reflection.

Take a deep breath, and let's start the *Love It* Process.

Give yourself plenty of time to fully process the questions below. This first step of this exercise asks you to go within and revisit a scene from your past where you noticed an imperfection. The second step invites deeper exploration to transform this self-limiting perception and to lean into love. The third part is to remove a love blocker by accepting an imperfection in someone else.

Step 1: Identify an imperfection

1. Think of a time in your life when you confronted an imperfection (real or imagined, seen or unseen) you saw in yourself. Name this event.

2. What did you identify as the imperfection?

3. Where were you at the time?

4. Was anyone else there with you? Who?

5. How did it make you feel to see this imperfection in yourself?

6. Was there anything that happened at that time or in the past to contribute to your feelings about yourself, related to this imperfection? What happened?

7. Did the experience trigger a self-limiting belief? What was it?

8. When you look back on that experience, do you think this imperfection may have served a purpose? If so, how did it help and/or hinder you?

9. What are the costs to you if you continue to give weight and meaning to the imperfection? What do you miss out on? What is the impact on you? And what is the impact on others?

Step 2: Transform the imperfection

1. Can you begin to accept the imperfection that you see in yourself? If so, what is it that you can accept?

2. If you cannot yet accept the imperfection or see that the imperfection is serving you, just take a few minutes and look back at your vision created in Chapter 4: *Dream It*. Notice your vision and see how the dream is within you and yet you still have the imperfection. Acknowledge that the dream and the imperfection co-exist. You can have one, both, or neither. You get to *Choose It*. So, choose powerfully. Write down how you feel when you witness this truth.

3. What has this imperfection taught you about yourself?

4. Close your eyes. Visualize yourself loving on the imperfection. Thank it for its contribution to your life. Thank it for the ways it makes you unique. Thank it for being there for you.

5. Allow your emotions to flow and be gentle with yourself. Allow love to flow to the space where the imperfection resides.

6. Now that you *Love It*, is the imperfection something you can change? If so, what step can you take to make the changes?

Step 3: Remove love blocks with others

1. Is there someone in your life with whom you would like to have a strong love connection but there is a block to that love? If so, who is it?

2. What is their imperfection (in your eyes) which is blocking the love connection? (Perhaps it is a personality trait, a habit, an attitude, a physical flaw, etc. Avoid projecting your self-limiting beliefs onto the person or their behavior. If you see that forgiveness is required for a behavior or action, go back to Chapter 3 and complete the *Forgive It* process with this person in mind.)

3. What can you accept about their imperfection?

4. What is available to you if you accept their imperfection?

5. What can acceptance teach you about the person and about yourself?

6. Now lean into love. Feel yourself accepting the imperfection.

Rinse. (Drink water.) Repeat the assignment until you have addressed other imperfections that you have confronted in your life and until you have accepted the imperfections of all people with whom you desire a strong love connection. And if you are ready to take your healing to another level, complete this process for those for whom you do not desire to have a love connection. This is an opportunity to practice unconditional love and allow the magnificent power of love to expand your life.

TIP: Self-care is about filling your cup . . . giving yourself what you need to live life to your fullest capacity. Forgiveness is self-care; loving yourself is self-care; and pursuing this path to wholeness . . . yup, it is also self-care. Be encouraged; you are caring for yourself simply by doing this work.

CHAPTER 7

Live It!

There are moments in life when you show up bigger than you know yourself to be. Maybe you can recall a time when you stood up for someone who was being mistreated. Or you marched in a demonstration to support an important cause. Or you took that leap you've been afraid to take.

What makes it possible to override resistance and just do it? The answer is *alignment*. This happens when your intention, your heart, your gifts, and your passions are aligned. At such times, the disempowering stories you've made up about your life are of no consequence; the masks, self-doubt, shame, and pain fall away. In these moments, you are in your wholeness. You are shining your light and *living your truth*.

You are put on this earth with an entelechy, a soul with a purpose to fulfill. Your purpose is to allow your spiritual self to be fully expressed in this physical realm. This purpose calls you to significance—to contribute something meaningful to others and for the greater good of all. Your purpose is to harness your energy and your unique gifts, talents, and passions to serve something greater than yourself. You are to live your life in communion with others to find your purpose, and then serve according to your purpose.

In her classic book, *A Return to Love*, Marianne Williamson famously said, "Our deepest fear is not that we are inadequate. Our deepest fear is that we are powerful beyond measure."[9]

> We deceive and disempower ourselves by thinking that we are weak, small, and inadequate. The truth is that we are strong, mighty, powerful, and energized by a tug on our lives to be all that we can be.

Your life force—the spirit that lives inside of you—is calling you to live the life intended for you. Its magnetic energy is strong; and when you acknowledge this pull and identify your purpose, there is no turning away from it. The universe will pull you toward everything and everyone aligned with your purpose, and you will be supplied with an abundance of resources to ensure that you can live this purpose.

With Power Tool 7: *Live It*, you will further explore what it means to live your life in an authentic way and how to fully embody your truth using all the power tools in your toolkit.

Just when I thought it all made sense, I got a sneak attack from shame, which caused me to learn an invaluable lesson about the importance of finding my voice and walking my talk on behalf of serving the greater good.

THE VOICE

The day I found my voice—wow! That was a miraculous moment of alignment for me . . . a life changer.

Despite the tremendous progress I had made during my four-year transformation journey up to that point, when my divorce was finalized in 2015, I found myself struggling to find my way out of the dark. The stress of my day-to-day life continued to be emotionally grueling. Several months later, my past and my present and the profound difficulty of the road ahead confronted me all at once. In despair, I cried out, "Why me?"

Days passed, and still no answer.

While driving to a client meeting, I was overcome with emotion. And again, I cried out in utter frustration, "Why me?"

After a moment of silence, I heard a voice. *Tonya, your journey is not yours alone. Share it with other people.*

Initially, I was shocked. I looked around for the person behind the voice.

When I realized I was alone, my body was still. Then the voice spoke: *Tonya, every tear you have cried, every heartbreak you have suffered, every pain you have felt, every illness you have been afflicted, every fall you have had . . . is NOT because you are weak. No. It's because you are strong, and your assignment is to share your story of overcoming these odds to help others overcome their own pain.*

Silence.

Then, the voice again, *The question to ask is, "Why not me?"*

Moments later, the stillness sparkled with excitement when I had the thought, *Wow! I have a book in me.*

That is when I vowed to write this book and to create a public platform to share what I had learned on my wholeness journey with you—the women of the world. I pledged to help you find your truth by evolving from shame and self-doubt to love and wholeness. As I began to write, I became clearer about my purpose and the benefit my stories have for serving the world. I believe that when you find your path to wholeness, you will naturally share your love with others. This is the nature of love . . . it desires to expand. And it is your highest purpose—to love. So, I declared that this book could cause a Global Love Revolution that would unite me and you to heal our pain, and then we'd be inspired to pass on this love to heal the suffering of the Earth.

The events happening in the United States in 2015 and 2016 were a pull on my heart. The country was torn apart by riots and protests in many cities due to the public exposure of police brutality against Black people. And there was a general atmosphere of hate, civil unrest, and divisiveness that got sparked during the presidential election. Shock waves spread around the globe, and citizens in many countries responded with their own messages. These events and many others during this time had contributed to an inescapable atmosphere of sadness, concern, anger, discord, and disruption.

Overcome with emotion, it was clear to me that my duty . . . my responsibility . . . my mission is to bring love to this troubled world. It was imperative that I call to women to rise to their fullest potential and power. With the awesome force of divine feminine energy, I have no doubt that we have all the love and vision it takes to heal the world.

Despite the intensity of my desire and no matter how much I was pulled to my mission and purpose, the start of the journey was a disappointment. I did not always perform my best. One of my top clients contracted with me for a significant speaking gig and I bombed. The gig was a flop. After the engagement, *I don't matter* laughed at me. "Ha, ha. So, you think you are going to change the world? You cannot even speak. You bombed. Sarah was right when she said 'You ain't all that.'"

Listening to the voice of my foundational belief was more of the same, a sabotage. I was embarrassed. I was unhappy. The experience was another big shame trigger. The wounded girl inside of me wanted to quit. On some level, I did quit. I turned my attention to things other than my dream and got derailed from the mission of sharing my message. I stopped speaking. I stopped writing this book.

Throughout my life, I've always had a contingent of friends, clients, and colleagues who believed in me. This came in handy at those times when I didn't believe in myself. They'd cheer me on and they'd hold me accountable to fulfill my commitments. As I faced the deep discouragement about my voice, my mastermind group of Jeff, John, and Eddie were relentless in their support. They gave me a powerful, emphatic nudge forward. Stated first by Jeff and then echoed by John and Eddie: "Enough with the excuses. The world is waiting for you to tell your story. The world is waiting for you to show up and lead. We are waiting for you to show up and lead."

Inspired by their encouragement and with my confidence somewhat restored, I went back to work on finding my voice. I hired a speaking coach and began practicing new techniques. I tried to get people to listen to what I had to say by speaking louder, but I still could not speak loud enough to be heard. I tried to get people to listen by being more physically demonstrative, and my voice still didn't seem to matter. I tried to put the right emotion into my words, and people still didn't seem to respond to me. I couldn't prove to myself that my voice mattered. Again, I felt defeated.

What was missing was the inner knowing that my voice matters—that I matter—regardless of what, when, where, or how I say something. I was looking outside myself for validation that I mattered. I was seeking approval, a cheering committee to say "that-a-girl."

As I was seeking my voice, I had to go inward. It was December 2019. I had fallen and fractured a bone in my left leg. With limited mobility, I was forced to rely on a wheelchair and crutches. I realized in this condition that it was cumbersome to perform my duties as an interior designer, and I conveniently used this "time out" to slow down and recalibrate my vision. During this period of stillness, I focused on my inward journey. Entering a meditative space, with a pen and my journal, I began writing everything that came into my mind. My reflections. My dreams. My desires. My vision. I concluded with this letter to myself:

Hello Darling T!

It appears that you are speaking but you don't believe what you are saying. Your words are consistent with what you believe and feel internally. And still, you seem to believe you are a fraud and an impostor. Is it possible that 'I don't matter' wants to win here?

Well, let go of your fears and embrace the wounded girl inside of you. You are safe, Little Toni. Lean into Grace. She's there to keep you safe. And don't forget that you are loved, strong, and capable.

You are meant to lead yourself and others on a journey toward self-discovery, self-awareness, and wholeness. Of course, you know this. I am just on the other side of your accomplishment and want to share with you that it serves you well to "BE" true to your natural leadership.

You have been on this journey for many years; and with each step, you have broken through barriers, raised the bar for yourself, had breakthroughs after breakdowns, and been a source of empowerment for others. You have reached higher with each step; and you have repeatedly debunked the self-limiting beliefs about your worth, value, power, and influence. And now, you have reached an even higher place in your transformation. At this new place, you are causing miracles on the planet because of your leadership, your giving spirit, and your authenticity. And you stand in this higher place now emboldened, strengthened, and inspired by the lessons learned and the new breakthroughs you've had on your journey.

You have connected with brilliant and amazing people around the world. You are a vessel of love and a haven for authenticity and empowered leadership for them. You have stepped out of your comfort zone to take on this Global Love Revolution, and for good cause. You have done this because it is your calling. You are THE ONE called to do this because YOU MATTER. You matter to the women who have healed because of you, and you matter to the world as it is experiencing the ripple effect of the love revolution you inspired. You are doing God's work; and your reward is "Well done!"

As the veil of healing blankets the earth, you fly higher. And you soar. Like the "Jane," you are when gliding on a zipline in the woods, you are free and empowered and connected and unapologetically courageous in your pursuit of this dream! Fly, Girl. It's your turn, and you got this!

Love,

Me

I had to acknowledge what was so. I had made the assignment bigger than me, and the shame I held was sabotaging it. Knowing that my call to fulfill my purpose was stronger than my wounded self, I had to befriend my shame, fall in love with myself, fall in love with my vision, fall in love with my purpose, and fall in love with how my voice could make a difference. Most importantly, I had to allow love to remind me to rise up and be the person who is a match for fulfilling my purpose. I had to accept the calling in my life that I am to serve women by sharing my story. And every day, I'd imagine myself living as if the life I dreamed of was already happening . . . as if this book was completed, as if I had already met the women I would be serving and we were journeying together in wholeness.

I desire to lead with grace and spread beauty and love around the world. When I had the a-ha moment and understood that my words and beliefs were misaligned, then I "got it." I heard it, I felt it, I saw it; it landed. My voice! I'd never heard it sound quite that way before, and it was beautiful. It wasn't the tone or the pitch or the cadence of my voice. It was the sound of confidence and inspiration and passion. If wholeness had a sound, that would be it.

What was next for me was to *Live It*.

So, there you have it. My voice expressed here in this book, *In High Heels on a Ladder: The 7 Power Tools for Designing Your Life*. This book is my movement of love. It is the result of completing my wholeness journey and living my dream, my purpose, my truth. I am putting it all on blast for one outrageously exciting opportunity: to cause a Global Love Revolution.

Live in your truth, live your purpose, and make a difference in the world. When you transform, you are given an opportunity to make a choice to be all that you can be, stop playing small, and step up to do all that you are called to do. It all depends on you. You have a say in how your life goes. You get to decide how big a light you want to shine. Life is for you; it is not against you. So, *Live It*.

POWER TOOL 7: LIVE IT

To live our purpose, we must befriend our shame.

It is natural to have doubts about how you can survive in the world in pursuit of your purpose when your shame has been with you for so long telling you otherwise about your abilities and how you fit in—or rather don't fit in—the world around you.

To find your voice and live on purpose, you must acknowledge the shame and self-doubt that keep you looking outside yourself for approval, rather than believing in yourself. Shame will not simply go away. There is no anti-shame remedy; there is no such thing as life before and life after shame. You can't divorce shame or put it in jail or bury it six feet under. Shame lives with you like an extra appendage. It is in your best interest to learn to live with it. Because of your inner work to rewrite the stories of your past and to reframe the shame, you are better equipped to deal with it, and you will have fewer breakdown experiences. Shame has less force, but it is there. Don't try to resist it or defend yourself against it, and don't apologize for it. When shame comes up, give it a warm embrace. Love shame for what it can teach you and use it as a cue to pivot and recalibrate.

We are source.

You have a say in how your life goes. You have a say in your joys and pains, your victories and losses, your courage and fears. Not only do you have a say, but you are the source!

This book is a reminder that to live a life of your own design, you must take command of the wheel and steer in the direction you want to go. I once heard a parable of a sailor and the wind. I cannot recall the source, but the essence of the story is that it doesn't matter how forceful the wind, it is the sailor who is in control of the sails to get him where he wants to go. You, Gorgeous, are in control of your life, despite whatever unexpected and unfavorable event life may present. You are the source of all that is your life.

Let's live our lives on purpose.

It is our human instinct to want to be the best we can be, not just for the sake of our own growth and potential fulfillment, but for the sake of our collective evolution. It is inherent in our nature to think of the well-being of others because of our shared humanity. What affects one, affects all.

Many of our great spiritual leaders have led movements that resulted in astonishing changes in our world. Mother Teresa served as "the voice for the poor," leading a movement to improve the lives of impoverished people. Nelson Mandela led the decades-long fight for civil rights and human equality for Blacks, with the ultimate victory being the emancipation of South Africa. Inspired by a dream of equality and a commitment to nonviolence, Dr. Martin Luther King, a prominent leader in the civil rights movement, helped to bring about the passage of laws that contributed to desegregation and anti-discrimination in America. And more recently, Malala Yousafzai has been honored as the youngest Nobel Peace Prize Laureate for her work as an advocate for girls' education and human rights.

Like Mother Teresa, Nelson Mandela, Dr. King, and Malala Yousafzai, we can choose to lead a movement to change the world. All movements start with one small step. It starts first with you. Then you pass it to him. He passes it to her. And she passes it to them. Before you know it, there is a movement. That movement shapes the world.

You don't need to have big aspirations like these global leaders to make a difference. And you don't have to be Mother Teresa, either. But you can do your part to inspire change in our world. You can do your part by standing in your truth.

> Find your purpose and share it with others in a way that serves you well and serves the greater good of all.

When you own the truth that you are love and you embody this love for yourself, it becomes easy to pass on love to your family, your friends, your community, your colleagues . . . all your circles of influence. When you walk in Unconditional Love, this causes a ripple effect of love that can spread over mountains, through valleys, and across rivers.

And Gorgeous, this ripple effect is what I mean by causing a Global Love Revolution. If a million women find wholeness through discovering the power to transcend their own shame and self-doubt, we can cause a movement of love that can heal the world of its pain.

So, when it comes to that story you made up about yourself, *Own It*. As for those experiences you encountered along your journey in life—you know the ones—*Choose It*. And as it relates to that thing you did and that person who did the other thing, *Forgive It*. Oh yeah! And that bold vision for your life, *Dream It*. As for that part of your soul that is beckoning you, *Become It*. You know that the truth of who you are that wants to set you free, *Love It*. The embodiment of all these Power Tools is in service to you, *Live It*—on purpose, wholly, according to your own design, and for the greater good of all.

JOURNEY TO WHOLENESS DESIGN SPACE: LIVE IT

DISCOVERY & PRACTICE

The practice of *Live It* asks you to embody all the principles and Power Tools you've put into practice in the preceding six chapters. This final reflection exercise will help you to build your level of awareness and give you the confidence to take your show on the road as an empowered person making a difference in the world. This self-review will enable you to recognize and celebrate what you've mastered in the journey to wholeness, as well as to identify which of the Power Tools need further attention and work. Review the information you have recorded in your journal for each of the chapters.

This is your time.

Choose a quiet, sacred place for this reflection where you can be undisturbed and where you feel free, comfortable, safe, and unencumbered by distractions. Find a seated position in which you feel most comfortable, either on a floor cushion or sitting on a sofa or chair. Have lots of drinking water and a box of tissues nearby. Feel free to light fragrance-free candles. Avoid stimulating your senses with visual information, music, incense, alcohol, cigarettes, or any potential distractions. The point is to drop into the space of reflection.

Take a deep breath. **Smile.** And let's start the *Live It* Process.

Step 1: Reflection

Give yourself plenty of time to review what you've learned about yourself over the course of your journey to wholeness practice in this book. Carefully study the reflection exercises you've completed for each of the chapters. Answer the questions below by charting the progress you've made in your journey with each of the 7 Power Tools by using a scale from 1 to 10 to measure your level of awareness from one (1) being little understanding or self-awareness to ten (10) being a high level of awareness and embodiment of that tool and principle.

Own It – The Power of Ownership

- Where are you now in the practice of "owning" your experience compared to where you were when you began this journey? *(Rate on scale of 1 to 10.)*
- What is the next step you could take to develop more mastery and practice of this Tool?

Choose It – The Power of Choice

- Where are you now in the practice of "choosing" your experience compared to where you were when you began this journey? *(Rate on scale of 1 to 10.)*
- What is the next step you could take to develop more mastery and practice of this Tool?

Forgive It – The Power of Forgiveness

- Where are you now in the practice of "forgiving" yourself and your perpetrators compared to where you were when you began this journey? *(Rate on scale of 1 to 10.)*

- What is the next step you could take to develop more mastery and practice of this Tool?

Dream It – **The Power of Visioning**

- Where are you now in the practice of "visioning" a life that you love compared to where you were when you began this journey? *(Rate on scale of 1 to 10.)*

- What is the next step you could take to develop more mastery and practice of this Tool?

Become It – **The Power of Living Your Purpose**

- Where are you now in the practice of "defining and living your purpose" compared to where you were when you began this journey? *(Rate on scale of 1 to 10.)*

- What is the next step you could take to develop more mastery and practice of this Tool?

Love It – **The Power of Love**

- Where are you now in the practice of "self-love and being a vessel of love" compared to where you were when you began this journey? *(Rate on scale of 1 to 10.)*

- What is the next step you could take to develop more mastery and practice of this Tool?

Live It – **The Power of Embodiment**

- Where are you now in the practice of "living life wholly by your design" compared to where you were when you began this journey? *(Rate on scale of 1 to 10.)*

- What is the next step you could take to develop more mastery and practice of this Tool?

Step 2: Empowerment

- What will your life look like when you are fully expressed and living a fully expanded life by your own design? *Consider: What parts of yourself are desiring to expand? What is available to you and others when you are fully expanded? Know that you have no limits. Your life desires its growth.*

- In Chapter 5, you defined the vision for your life; and in Chapter 6, you defined the purpose of your life. Review the work you completed in these chapters.

- What might be the first five steps you can take to move yourself in the direction of your dreams? *What is needed from you? Don't worry about the "how." The universe will take care of that.*

- What might be the first five steps you can take to satisfy the calling on your life? *What is needed from you? Don't worry about the "how." Leave that up to the universe.*

- Are you willing to fulfill your purpose for the greater good of all? Why? *Again, don't worry about the "how." The universe has that part covered.*

Start immediately taking those first steps. *Live It!*

The End Is Really a New Beginning . . .

HELLO GORGEOUS!

Congratulations, you've done it! You have completed the journey in this book. If you have put yourself completely in, you have found your truth and this truth has set you free! Your hard work deserves to be acknowledged and celebrated. Applaud yourself for the effort you've put into your journey to wholeness.

If you still have some work to do to complete the journey, I acknowledge you for your effort and all that you have learned and accomplished. Whatever this journey has exposed for you, accept and bless it for the lessons you learned and for the light it shined on your truth. What you have learned and discovered is only part of your story of becoming . . . it is a beautiful start on the journey to wholeness.

This book is designed for you to return for guidance whenever and wherever you may need support along your journey. This isn't a "one and done" read. You can work on the Power Tools as often as needed in your evolution.

Before you started this journey, you were likely wearing some mask du jour, trying to evade some pain and shame in the quest to find the missing thing that may have been hiding in plain sight. Now, you are empowered with tools and have designed a life you love by understanding and accepting your past, embracing forgiveness and dreaming, loving yourself and your purpose, and committing to living a life by your own design and for the greater good of all.

Please don't be dismayed by the inevitable sneak attack from your old life. Your foundational beliefs are not going to simply disappear. Your power over their influence rests in your commitment to living a well-designed life and keeping yourself spiritually grounded in the strength of the Power Tools and the practices which support them. And most importantly, when you live in your purpose, embrace the "you" you become to fulfill that purpose, and lean into your love, there is no telling what you can do.

Because we—you and me—have journeyed together, we are united as one. In this spirit of oneness, I'd like to invite you to join me on a mission to help heal the world. Now that you have completed the work in this book, you can pass on your love and wisdom to your circles of influence. Can you say "yes" to that? Can you *Live It*—your truth—for the greater good of all?

I'd like you to stand firmly in your wholeness. And from this place, spread love within your family and community. Be the source of healing for others. This means accepting others as they are, forgiving their transgressions, understanding that they may be blinded by self-limiting beliefs, and granting them your grace and compassion. The more people who experience your love, the more healing we will spread around the globe.

Will you join me in this Global Love Revolution? If a million women find wholeness by discovering their power to overcome the pain of shame and self-doubt as you have, we can work together in a movement to heal the world.

To learn more about the Global Love Revolution, please visit tonyacomer.com. Sign up for my mailing list to learn about additional training opportunities and to get updates on events to globalize this cause.

Well done, Gorgeous! I will see you real soon!

With all my love,

Tonya "Toni" Comer

Your Spiritual Sister on Your Journey to Wholeness

KEY TAKEAWAYS

In and of themselves, the things that happen in your life have no meaning. It's your response to these events and the stories you project onto them that give them their meaning.

—Chapter 1 *Own It* Page 24

Your foundational belief is like an anchor holding you in place; it feels impossible to change—like an undeniable, unrelenting truth. And you then hold on to this belief like you're serving a life sentence—a form of punishment for a crime for which you have been found guilty.

—Chapter 1 *Own It* Page 27

You live in a fabricated reality with a negative self-image and a false identity, believing these things to be your truth. The real truth is that you made it all up.

—Chapter 1 *Own It* Page 30

You will never be defeated if you make the choice to take the seed of good from every experience—no matter how traumatic, strange, inconceivable, challenging, or dark.

—Chapter 2 *Choose It* Page 56

Shame gets attached to your identity and lives with you—in you—as a truth. Really though, shame is not the truth; it is merely residue of an emotional trauma.

—Chapter 3 *Forgive It* Page 69

To refuse someone forgiveness only shackles you to the hurt and shame you experienced, and it holds you hostage to the perpetrator. When you forgive the perpetrator, you disentangle the emotions of pain, blame, and shame from the event. And you free yourself.

—Chapter 3 *Forgive It* Page 71

Recognizing our common humanity makes it easy to feel compassion for yourself and others, and it opens the door to self-forgiveness.

—Chapter 3 *Forgive It* Page 75

Forgiveness is a power move—an act of love and grace that comes from the wisdom of an open heart.

—Chapter 3 *Forgive It* Page 77

You can direct your mind toward thoughts that kill the dream, or you can direct positive energy toward visualizing the dream. You have a choice. Why not choose to dream?

—Chapter 4 *Dream It* Page 96

Dreaming empowers you to access your heart by discovering the things you love and most desire.

—Chapter 4 *Dream It* Page 96

You can't just put a spit-shine on your shame and buff out the painful experiences that marked you. This pain must be acknowledged for you to get the strength you need to grow beyond it.

—Chapter 5 *Become It* Page 114

When you find your purpose, your first thought will not be a denial, "Oh, but I am invisible . . . not lovable . . . not worthy of it . . . " Your first thought will likely be empowered, inspired, and positive. It will be followed by a big fat, "Yes!"

—Chapter 5 *Become It* Page 116

Love is an infectious, contagious energy. You cannot help but want to share it with others and they cannot help but want to share it with you.

—Chapter 6 *Love It* Page 130

Our imperfections shine a light on the truth.

—Chapter 6 *Love It* Page 132

When you do the work to accept your imperfections, your love expands—it wraps itself around you in a long embrace and teaches you to love yourself and others in the most profound way.

—Chapter 6 *Love It* Page 132

When you choose love, you choose the good life.

—Chapter 6 *Love It* Page 134

We deceive and disempower ourselves by thinking that we are weak, small, and inadequate. The truth is that we are strong, mighty, powerful, and energized by a tug on our lives to be all that we can be.

—Chapter 7 *Live It* Page 142

Find your purpose and share it with others in a way that serves you well and serves the greater good of all.

—Chapter 7 *Live It* Page 150

References

1. Oxford Languages Dictionary Online, Oxford University Press, 2023. https://www.oxfordreference.com/display/10.1093/oi/authority.20110803115639406;jsessionid=8119EC685D5AA1B-0F631AFAF8AA5C67D

2. Oprah Winfrey and Bruce D. Perry M.D. Ph.D., *What Happened to You? Conversations on Trauma, Resilience, and Healing,* Flatiron Books, 1st Edition, April 2021.

3. Viktor E Frankl, *Man's Search for Meaning,* 26th Printing, Beacon Press, 2006, Pages 65-66.

4. Brené Brown, *I Thought It Was Just Me (But It Wasn't): Making the Journey from "What Will People Think? To I Am Enough,* Penquin Random House LLC, 2008, p. 5.

5. Abraham H. Maslow, *A Theory of Human Motivation,* (reprinted from the 1943 edition) Martino Fine Books, 2013.

6. M. B. Frothingham, *Fight, Flight, Freeze, or Fawn: What This Response Means.* Simply Psychology. 2021, Oct 06. www.simplypsychology.org/fight-flight-freeze-fawn.html

7. Gary Chapman, *The 5 Love Languages: The Secret to Love That Lasts,* Northfield Publishing, Reprint edition, January 1, 2010.

8. Jean Houston, *The Hero and The Goddess: The Odyssey As Mystery and Initiation,* Ballantine Books, 1992, p. 52.

9. Marianne Williamson, *A Return to Love: Reflections on the Principles of a Course in Miracles,* HarperCollins Publishers, 1992, p. 165.

Acknowledgements

I'd have to write another book just to express the depth of my gratitude for the many people who have played a role in my own journey to wholeness and in my path to authorship. In lieu of that, I summarize my appreciation. Please know, though, that these words pale in comparison to the appreciation and love I hold in my heart for all of you.

I express my deepest gratitude for all the people who served as perpetrators in my life and for the less-than-desirable but oh-so-necessary circumstances in my life. You have served me in a way that glamour, gold, and glory could never have. Your role in my life shaped me into a person who is courageous enough to author this book and has evolved through pain to find her purpose. Thank you for the trials and the opportunity to prevail.

Thank you to all who have encouraged me throughout this process—and there are so many of you. At times, I've had to lean in to your belief that I could author this book when I couldn't trust my own. Thank you for your enthusiasm and for believing in me. I am infinitely grateful to you.

To my editor Kendra Langeteig, Ph.D. (edgewisepublishing.com), you had me at "Hello." A transformational book doctor you most certainly are. Yes, you did all the editor stuff. Yes, you took my words and concept and lovingly scrutinized it from every vantage point. Yes, you helped me elevate the book to match my vision. Yes, you did all of that extraordinarily well. And what you did that made it all successful was you GOT ME. This is our recipe for success and sisterhood. You are an angel whose wings carried me through. I celebrate and thank you for all of that and everything.

To my Dream Team, the extraordinary folks at Steve Harrison Publishing's Author Success Program (authorsuccess.com), I sing your praises. You paved the way for me to have this victory. Special shout out to Steve Harrison for your infinite wisdom and for always having the right resource and the right solution. I cannot thank you enough. A notable mention to my book coach Trish Ahjel Roberts. Your own juicy life journey was a magnet for our successful partnership. Thank you for helping me to navigate the maze of work from manuscript to production. Soul sisters forever! To Valerie Costa, Kimberlie Cruse, Maggie McLaughin, and Cristina Smith, thank you for sharing your gifts and patience as I navigated the production phase of book development. And Christy Day, your instinct regarding the interior design was spot on! We had to kick it into high gear to make it across the finish line. But we did it! I am grateful for your winning spirit. Steven Scholl, thank you for your keen vision to see words and not-so-words. I am grateful for your scrutinizing eye. And to Joe McAllister, what can I say? You simply rock!

To Jack Canfield (jackcanfield.com), who saw the Chicken Soup for the Soul® story in my life, thank you for reading this book and for your endorsement. I'm grateful for your support, thoughtfulness, and encouragement; and I am inspired by your wisdom.

To Andrew Janssen (bhaudio.com), I am over-the-moon grateful for your enthusiastic support and unparalleled "commitment to the process." You, Sir, are a genius! You stepped in at the final hours and gave invaluable feedback on the book. You took time and care to read each word and check that all "i"s were dotted and "t"s were crossed. And then you stepped up as the perfect maestro, directing all aspects of the production of my audio book. I marvel at you and your many talents. I am truly grateful for your kindness, thoughtfulness, and generosity. And a big fat thank you is hailed for your "Woo."

To the lovely Betsy Harmatz (bhaudio.com), one of the most miraculous things to witness on this great planet is when a spontaneous connection forms almost as if by a seeming wave of a magic wand. I am convinced that the abracadabra that caused our partnership was perfectly aligned by divine intervention. I am thrilled that I got to meet you and work with you on this all-important work for women. Your thoughtfulness has made a lasting impression on my heart. Your radiance gives me many reasons to smile, and your talent has produced a beautiful audio book. I treasure the moments and you!

To the beautiful Sarah Jane Janssen, who knew that on one wacky night of absolute desperation, you'd answer a call to be a proofreading lifeline? I am extraordinarily grateful that you said, "Yes." You are a godsend. I appreciate everything you did to contribute to the editing of this book. May you embrace your superpower and use it to continue to do great things in this world.

To James Smith, Jr. Ph.D. (drjamessmithjr.com), thank you for believing in the "little girl from the projects." You gave me a leaning post at a time when I couldn't hold up my own weight. And you reminded me of the power of my own vulnerability. I have indeed been "Jimpacted." For all of this, I am eternally grateful to you.

To my friend John E. Thomas (coach2create.com), this whole thing started with me in the car and you on the phone. You scribed my first thoughts for this book. While it has evolved and blossomed since then, you played an integral part and watched this dream spark and take shape. Thank you for the long conversations as I continued to press the limits—mine and yours—and the karaoke nights to recharge after.

To photographer Dan Naylor (dannaylor.com), I thoroughly enjoyed working with you to shoot the photos for the book cover. You were the first person on this planet who knew my full vision for this book and your enthusiastic response is unforgettable. Thank you for celebrating me through your lens and your heart.

To Mikey Matchesky, thank you for working with me to lay out the book cover. I am grateful that you're on Team Tonya. I love seeing your evolution as you continue to reach new heights in your graphic design career. You're a godsend.

To Brigitte Kolibab, thank you for the many early morning, midafternoon, and late-night brainstorming sessions we had to reimagine this book project. You are a beautiful presence in my life and have been a wonderful contribution to my wholeness journey. Thank you for everything!

To Karen T., thank you for caring enough to challenge me to be my best. I am forever comforted by your love and influence in my life. There aren't enough words for "Thank you!"

To Ron Adolph, words are minuscule in comparison to the gratitude I hold in my heart for you. You've been a beacon of hope at a time when I was in my darkest place. You've taught me lessons about integrity. You've shown me the power of falling and getting back up. You've shown me what leadership looks like. You've demonstrated what true love looks like. And you were the first person to guide me to this world of transformation. I hope the work I do in this world makes you proud. I am grateful to call you my friend.

To Ken Canion (coachkencanion.com), thank you for being an unapologetic advocate of women—and all people for that matter. And thank you for believing in me and encouraging me on my quest to live my best life. *The Biggest Loser* may have been the winning formula for your success in your health domain, but your heart is the secret sauce to your widely successful career as a raw, real, and relatable coach. I appreciate you and your inspiration.

To my family at the National Speakers Academy Philadelphia Chapter, thank you for your wildly enthusiastic endorsement of the book's title and for being in the brainstorm with me. I am grateful to you Brandon Blackburn-Dwyer, Gerry Lantz, Theresa McGlinchey, Bill Relyea, Tarnissha Sass, Ken Shur, Paul Sloate, Rod Wallace, Rita Wilkins, and Matthew Zaun.

To my global mastermind family Yasmin El Baggari, Nezha Larhrissi, Kavitha Manevannan, Marc Phillippe, and Diego Taira, thank you for holding me high and believing in my dream. Your support means the world to me. I love you all more than you know.

To Jeff Cohen, Eddie Gorman, and John Harper, it was a journey of a thousand miles. And you were by my side the entire time. I love and appreciate you more than you will ever know.

Thank you to all the many teachers, coaches, and healers I've met along my life's journey. I cannot imagine the direction my life would have gone if I hadn't received your support, wisdom, direction, and sometimes even your push. Celebrate yourself for what you've given me. Because it meant so much, I've committed to paying it forward.

Thank you to those I love who have been mentioned in this book for allowing me to acknowledge your influence in my life's journey. Mama, my sister Boo, Angel, Katie, Kai, Mr. Genius, Sanjay, Danny, Jordan, Jay, Gary, Tené, Bill, Betty, Jeff, John, and Eddie, I appreciate you and love you forever!

To the lovely Sudanna Morris, I am blessed that my journey led me to you. You've been a beautiful presence of grace in my life. On the latter part of this book journey, you've watched me test things out, reinvent everything, overthink most things, rewrite and rewrite and rewrite some more, ask the same questions twice maybe even three times, laugh at myself, gasp at my mistakes, rebound from setbacks, and get to the finish line. Through it all, you just ebbed and flowed. Thank you for your steadiness, easiness, grace, and enthusiastic support.

To my godchildren—the children I never birthed but have taken some claim—you will never know how much you inspire me. I am blessed to be your Auntie. Since you were just wee little things, each of you has been the apple in my eye. I am proud to watch you grow and navigate life in your own way, on your own terms. May you always know your own power to create the life of your dreams. Justin, Brian, Olivia, Victoria, Anand, Brandon, Amit, and Kennadie, I love you with all my heart.

To my tribe . . . my sisterhood . . . my dearly beloveds, we've gathered here together to get through this thing called "life." Janet Christian, Pamela Crunkleton, Liane Godfrey, Jill Jones, Dilia Wood, Dianne Martin, and Robin Smith, you've showed up for me in your own way. Thank you for the laughter, the tears, the hugs, the figuring things out, the "oh, no he didn't," the cheerleading, the stargazing, the dream building, the adventure taking, the ride or die. Thank you for all of it. My love for you runs deep.

To my Navin, it would take a lifetime to tell you how much you mean to me. I leave you with this: My heart is full of the love I have for you.

I am so blessed to have had wonderful clients and client relationships. To all of you, you have all been with me on my journey and have contributed uniquely to my life and success. A special shout out to Carole, Darnell, Edda, Gwen, Hope, Linsey, Lydia, James, Jela, Juanita, and Regine. You have shown me so much love, loyalty, and grace. It is through serving you that I have come to know my true value.

To my entire family and my extended group of friends, I take you on this journey with me. May we learn, grow, heal, and love together. I love you forever and always.

To my very first superhero, my Mama, this book is my version of standing on the mountain top and declaring to the world, "I owe my life to my Mama." I carry on your legacy with the little nuggets of wisdom I share with the women I serve. Thank you for your example. I love you with all of my heart.

My deepest gratitude extends to my beloved sister, Boo. Just weeks before I was ready to take this book to print, you took your last breath. I have allowed your death—and its pain—to crack me open. And in this open space, I find more room to heal and to grow. And most especially, I find more room to love. I take this love and give it to others. And I do it in your honor. As you rest in spirit, I hope you find the same joy you had as a child when we'd skip around singing "Skidamarink a dink a dink, Skidamarink a doo, I love you." It's an old memory . . . one I hope to never forget. I love you forever and always.

To all of the gorgeous people who embark on this wholeness journey and become part of the Global Love Revolution, I thank you in advance for your willingness to be courageous, inspiring, generous, and loving. Our planet is a better place because of your contribution and commitment. I stand in awe of you!

About the Author

TONYA COMER has been named one of the Top 20 African American Interior Designers in the United States by the Black Interior Designers Network. She is principal of the boutique interior design firm, Tonya Comer Interiors, founded in 2007. Her award-winning product designs have sold around the globe. She has also won awards for the roles she's served as a community and business thought leader. As a global transformational leader, she serves as a speaker and workshop presenter helping people design their lives.

Tonya holds an MBA from Michigan State University's Eli Broad Graduate School of Management and a BA from Duquesne University. She studied interior design at London Metropolitan University. Tonya formerly worked in broadcasting and served many roles in corporate America.

When asked as a seven-year-old what she wanted to be when she grew up, Tonya said, "I want to spread love around the world." Today, she spreads her message of love as an author, speaker, and LIFEdesign coach dedicated to helping women find the path from shame and self-doubt to self-love and wholeness. And when she isn't doing all of that, Tonya Comer is an adventure-seeking, rollercoaster-loving, jump-out-of-a-plane-first spirit who lives life out loud.